The Complete Greek Tragedies
Edited by David Grene and Richmond Lattimore

Aeschylus II

The Suppliant Maidens
Translated by S. G. Benardete

The Persians
Translated by S. G. Benardete

Seven Against Thebes
Translated by David Grene

Prometheus Bound
Translated by David Grene

WASHINGTON SQUARE PRESS
POCKET BOOKS • NEW YORK

The Complete Greek Tragedies

AESCHYLUS II

University of Chicago Press edition published November, 1956

WASHINGTON SQUARE PRESS edition published July, 1967
3rd printing........................March, 1972

L

Published by
POCKET BOOKS, a division of Simon & Schuster, Inc.,
630 Fifth Avenue, New York, N.Y.

WASHINGTON SQUARE PRESS editions are distributed
in the U.S. by Simon & Schuster, Inc., 630 Fifth Avenue,
New York, N.Y. 10020 and in Canada by Simon & Schuster of Canada, Ltd., Richmond Hill, Ontario, Canada.

·60

The widely acclaimed
University of Chicago editions of

THE COMPLETE
GREEK TRAGEDIES

Edited by
David Grene and Richmond Lattimore

A complete collection of the tragedies of Aeschylus, Sophocles, and Euripides rendered in modern translations reflecting a rare fidelity to the spirit, the rhythm, and the meaning of the original texts.

AESCHYLUS I—*Oresteia*
Agamemnon/The Libation Bearers/The Eumenides

AESCHYLUS II
The Suppliant Maidens/The Persians/Seven against Thebes/Prometheus Bound

SOPHOCLES I
Oedipus the King/Oedipus at Colonus/Antigone

SOPHOCLES II
Ajax/The Women of Trachis/Electra/Philoctetes

EURIPIDES I
Alcestis/The Medea/The Heracleidae/Hippolytus

EURIPIDES II
The Cyclops/Heracles/Iphigenia in Tauris/Helen

EURIPIDES III
Hecuba/Andromache/The Trojan Women/Ion

EURIPIDES IV
Rhesus/The Suppliant Women/Orestes/Iphigenia in Aulis

EURIPIDES V
Electra/The Phoenician Women/The Bacchae

GENERAL INTRODUCTION

THIS volume contains the other four plays of Aeschylus not included in Richmond Lattimore's version of the *Oresteia*. With these two volumes a complete English Aeschylus is before the reader.

Each of these four plays was a part of a trilogy of which the other members have been lost. Necessarily, therefore, none of them has the completeness of effect which is so marked in the *Oresteia*. Furthermore, only in the *Prometheus* have we much evidence concerning the other two plays of the trilogy, and even here what we know is hardly enough to make us certain whether that one of the trilogy known to us as *Prometheus the Fire Bearer* is the first or the last of the series. Our *Seven against Thebes* is the last of a trilogy dealing with Laius, Oedipus, and his sons, but we have no sure indication as to the character of the other plays.

Quite apart from their individual merits, reading these four plays broadens the understanding of Aeschylus too frequently based on a knowledge of the *Oresteia* and sometimes of the *Agamemnon* alone. They reveal his range as a dramatic author and his extraordinary originality, both in style and thought, seen in the context of the rest of the Greek tragedies. There is a bewildering difference between the four plays in style and form, and this has necessarily cost the volume the uniformity achieved in the translation of the *Oresteia*. Here the variations must be transmitted in English in some intelligible relation to the Greek. In *The Suppliant Maidens* and *The Persians* much that is hard to render in English lies in an area where thought and expression melt into one another so that it appears impossible to capture the original, or approach it, in another tongue. The

Seven against Thebes is a fierce, archaic play which to us appears largely melodramatic and even to its contemporaries, or at least to the succeeding generation, seemed stiff and overcolored. It is hard not to render it at times into a bombastic Wardour Street English, and often no great injustice is done to the Greek if so rendered. The *Prometheus* is perhaps most difficult of all. Both vocabulary and expression are relatively simple. Parts are downright prosy, but the great passages are of the highest flights of Greek dramatic poetry. I have rendered into prose parts which seemed to me intolerable in any strictly formalized medium in English. The majestic note is beyond the range of anyone not as great as its author. I am well aware of the inadequacies of this version. Its only merit may be that it is very literal, and when it cannot convey the spirit of the Greek, it perhaps suggests to the imaginative reader a direction in which to look.

DAVID GRENE

CONTENTS

THE
SUPPLIANT MAIDENS

Translated by S. G. Benardete

INTRODUCTION TO
THE SUPPLIANT MAIDENS

IT HAD always been thought by modern scholars that *The Suppliant Maidens* was the earliest Greek play still preserved, and the date of its production was given as *circa* 490 B.C. This opinion was based on stylistic considerations as well as on the fact that the protagonist of the play is the chorus itself, which Aristotle tells us to have been the early condition of the drama. A papyrus recently published, however, would seem to suggest that the trilogy, of which *The Suppliant Maidens* is the first part, was first produced after 470 B.C. Should this prove to be the case, it will be a real puzzle why Aeschylus kept the play in his drawer for twenty years; for it is hardly likely that he should have reverted to the archaism of *The Suppliant Maidens* after having written *The Persians*.

The plot of the play is simple. The fifty daughters of Danaus, descendants of the Argive Io, flee from Egypt to Argos because their Egyptian cousins wish, without their consent, to marry them. They come to a sacred grove near Argos, where the rest of the action takes place. Pelasgus, the King of Argos, is unwilling to grant them sanctuary unless the populace seconds his request; and the populace, convinced by the king and their own father, does grant it. But it is not a moment too soon; for after the maidens hear they are saved, their father informs them that the Egyptian cousins are just landing, and while he goes to bring aid, a herald of their cousins comes to take them away. Pelasgus, however, returns with an armed force, and the herald, threatening war, is forced to withdraw. Then Danaus returns again,

2

counseling them to behave decently, and the play ends with a song of deliverance. Since the second and third parts of the trilogy are lost, and only a few scattered notices of the plot remain, we cannot be certain what Aeschylus' purpose was. In the second play the maidens were somehow forced to marry their cousins (perhaps because Pelasgus dies), but they swear to their father to kill them on their wedding night. All except Hypermnestra fulfil their oath, while she— "splendide mendax," Horace calls her—out of love for her husband saves him. In the last play Hypermnestra is forced to stand trial because she violated her oath; and in a scene reminiscent of that in the *Eumenides*, Aphrodite herself appears and defends her. Part of her speech survives:

As the sacred heaven longs to pierce the earth,
So love takes hold of earth to join in marriage,
And showers, fallen from heaven brought to bed,
Make the earth pregnant; and she in turn gives birth
To flocks of sheep and Ceres' nourishment—
A marriage that drenches the springtime of the woods—
For all this I am in part responsible.

The Suppliant Maidens is an international play. The Danaids are refugees, Greeks by descent, Egyptians in appearance (ll. 234–37, 277–90, 496 ff.), and according to Egyptian law they have no legal right to refuse to marry their cousins. For when Pelasgus wishes to know what right they have, the maidens in reply only declare their hatred of their cousins, implying by their evasion of the question the absence of any legal claim to his protection (ll. 387–91). Thus both by nature and by law they are defenseless. If they really looked like Greeks, as well as were Greeks by an obscure genealogy, and if they had some legal justification, Pelasgus might have been willing to take up their defense without the consent of the people; but once it becomes a case of pure or natural justice independent of all legality, with the maidens' arbitrary dislike of their cousins their only motive, Pelasgus must defer to the will of the people. Since the maidens insist upon the rights of the will alone, Pelasgus allows in turn the people's will to sanction it and make it law. In the second play the oath of the Danaids becomes law, and Hypermnestra, in violating it, repeats her sisters' original defiance of Egyptian law; but as on this occasion it is not a human law that she has betrayed, a goddess must justify her conduct. Aphrodite insists upon the prerogatives of love, a force that transcends even the sacredness of oaths. Thus the trilogy is complete. At first the Egyptians embodied law, though strangely enough lust also supported them, while the Danaids represented a freedom that was not bound by any positive enactments. But once this freedom has been approved by law, Hypermnestra alone remains outside it; and as she cannot be defended merely by a democratic procedure, a universal divine law, more authoritative than even the people's will, must rescue her. Having only the first part of the trilogy, we cannot be confident that Aeschylus' purpose was exactly this; but the claims of the city as opposed to claims still more powerful would seem to underlie the play, claims that at each stage become more contrary to one another and more difficult to resolve.

The Suppliant Maidens as a play is not very exciting, and we can easily see why the chorus was later abandoned as the protagonist. A chorus can convey only a lyrical mood; it can hardly support any genuine passion. The Danaids, for example, say they are frightened when the Egyptians are coming, but we do not believe them: their songs, divided into strophe and antistrophe,* betray their detachment, and they always talk more like commentators on their actions than like the actors themselves. Although the choruses of *The Suppliant Maidens* are some of the most beautiful Aeschylus ever wrote, the dialogue seems extremely artificial and forced, with the air of set speeches directed more to the audience than to the other actors. *The Persians,* on the other

---

* Throughout this play and *The Persians*, strophes and antistrophes are marked by the symbols — and = respectively.

hand, suffers from the opposite fault: the speeches, even though long, are dramatic, while the choral songs are far inferior to those of *The Suppliants*. Only in the *Oresteia* did Aeschylus achieve a perfect balance between them.

CHARACTERS

Chorus of maidens, daughters of Danaus

Danaus, their father

Pelasgus, King of Argos

Herald of Egyptians, cousins to the Danaans

6

THE SUPPLIANT MAIDENS

SCENE: *A sacred grove near Argos, adorned with statues of Greek gods.*

Chorus
Zeus Protector, protect us with care.
From the subtle sand of the Nile delta
Our ship set sail. And we deserted:
From a holy precinct bordering Syria
We fled into exile, condemned
Not for murder by a city's decree,
But by self-imposéd banishment abhorring
Impious marriage with Egyptus' sons.   10

Danaus, father, adviser and lord,
Setting the counters of hope,
Picked the smallest pawn of grief,
Quickly to fly through the sea,
And find anchor at Argos,
Whence we boast to descend,
By the breathing caress of Zeus
On a cow driven wild.

With suppliant olive branch,
To what kinder land could we turn?   20

Whose city, whose earth and bright water,
Olympian gods, ancient gods below
Possessing the tomb, and Zeus Savior,
Keeper of pious men, receive
(Respectful the air of this land)
These suppliant maidens well.

7

But that thick swarm of insolent men,   30
Before ever landing in this swamp waste,
Return them and their ship to the sea;
And by the winter sting of hurricane,
Facing the wild sea, by thunder and lightning,
By rain-winds may they die;
Before appropriating what law forbids,
Cousins to lie on unwilling beds.   40

Now I invoke
The calf of Zeus Avenger
Beyond the sea:
A child from grazing
Cow, genetrix,
Held by the breath of Zeus,
Born with a fateful name:
Epaphus, Caress.—

Him I invoke:
In pastures here our mother
Suffered before: 50
I'll show a witness
Faithful but unex-
pected to natives here.
They shall know the truth
At last and at length.=

And if some neighbor here knows bird cries,
Hearing our bitter passion he will think
He hears the hawk-chased, sad bird Metis,   60
The wife of Tereus,—
                    Who weeps with passion
Barred from rivers and the countryside;
Who sang a child's death-dirge, whom she killed,
Perverse her wrath.=

Thus melancholy I
With Ionian songs
Eat my Nile-soft cheek,

8

My heart unused to tears.   70
We gather blooms of sorrow,
Anxious if a friend,
Someone, will protect us,
Exiles from a misty land.—

But gods ancestral, hear!
Behold justice kindly.
Truly hating pride
Grant nothing undecreed: 80
So just you'd be to marriage.
Even war has havens,
Bulwark for the weary
Exile, a respect of gods. =

May his will, if it's Zeus's, be well,
His will not easily traced.
Everywhere it gleams, even in blackness,
With black fortune to man.—

And so certain it falls without slips,   90
By sign of Zeus fulfilled.
Dark are the devices of his counsel,
His ways blind to our sight. =

From towered hopes
He casts men destructive,
No violence
He armors.
All providence
Is effortless: throned,
Holy and motionless,
His will is accomplished.—   100

On mortal pride
Look down, how it waxes
And flourishes
By marriage
Remorselessly:

Intent in its frenzy,
Spur inescapable,
Deceived to destruction.= 110

I sing suffering, shrieking,
Shrill and sad am weeping,
My life is dirges
And rich in lamentations,
Mine honor weeping.
   I invoke your Apian land,
   You know my foreign tongue.
   Often I tear my Sidonian veils.— 120

We grant gods oblations
Where all is splendid
And death is absent.
O toils undecipherable!
Where lead these billows?
   I invoke your Apian land.
   You know my foreign tongue.
   Often I tear my Sidonian veils.= 130

Linen-bound ship, secure from the sea,
With fair winds brought me;
Nor do I blame.
May Father, timely omniscient,
Perfect a gracious end, that 140
   Seeds mighty of solemn mother
   Escape, O woe,
   Unwed, virgin to the bed of man.—

Daughter of Zeus pure, may she behold,
Who guards walls sacred,
Willing my will.
May virgin, rescuing virgins,
In all her power come, that 150
   Seeds mighty of solemn mother
   Escape, alas,
   Unwed, virgin to the bed of man.=

But if not,
A sunburnt race
Shall go beseeching
To Zeus of the dead
(Gracious to strangers),
Hanging ourselves,
If gods Olympian heed not.   160
   O Zeus! Sought out by the gods,
   By snake-hate of Io:
   I know Hera's madness
   Conquering all.
   Winter comes by sharp winds.—

Then Zeus in
Injustice hates
His son begotten,
And that is unjust: 170
Face now averted
Away from my prayers.
But would that Zeus hearken!
   O Zeus! Sought out by the gods,
   By snake-hate of Io:
   I know Hera's madness
   Conquering all.
   Winter comes by sharp winds.=

Danaus
Prudence, my daughters; prudently you came
With an agèd father as your trusted pilot.
And now, with foresight, I advise your taking
Care to seal my words within your mind.
I see dust, the silent clarion of arms,   180
But not in silence are the axles turned;
Crowds I see, armed with shield and spear,
Followed by horses and curvèd chariots.
Perhaps the princes of this land have come
To meet us, informed by messenger;
But whether kindly purposed or provoked
To savageness they speed their armament,

11

Here it is best to act the suppliant,
This rock, this altar of assembled gods,
Stronger than ramparts, a shield impenetrable.   190
Now quickly prepare white suppliant wreaths,
Sign of Zeus sacred, held in the left hand;
Mournful, respectful, answer needfully
The strangers; tell distinctly of an exile
Unstained by murder. Let nothing bold
Attend your voice, and nothing vain come forth
In glance but modesty and reverence.
Not talkative nor yet a laggard be in speech: 200
Either would offend them. Remember to yield:
You are an exile, a needy stranger,
And rashness never suits the weaker.

Chorus
With prudence, father, you speak to the prudent.
I shall keep a watch on your discreet commands.
May Zeus, my ancestor, look on us.

Danaus
May he look then with propitious eye.

Chorus
Now would I wish to be near your side.

Danaus
Delay not.

Chorus
        O Zeus, compassion ere we die.   210

Danaus
If Zeus is willing, this will end well.
And now that bird of Zeus invoke.

Chorus
Preserving rays of the sun we call.

Danaus
Call on Apollo, the god, who from heaven once fled.

Chorus
So knowing this fate, may he have compassion.

Danaus
Let him be compassionate, defend us with care.

Chorus
What other gods must I invoke?

Danaus

                I see
This trident, a God's symbol.

Chorus

               Who brought us
Here well: may he receive us now well.

Danaus
And that is another Hermes, a Greek custom.   220

Chorus
May he be a good herald to those who are free.

Danaus
All gods here at a common altar worship.
Settle on the sacred ground like doves
Clustering together, fearing the winged hawks,
Who hatefully pollute their very blood.
Bird consumes bird, how could it be pure?
How, unwilling brides, myself unwilling,
Could they be pure? Who not even in hell,
Where another Zeus among the dead (they say)   230
Works out their final punishment, can flee
Their guilt of lust. Fix your eye on that
In answer, that victory be with you well.

       (*Enter the King of Argos and company.*)

King
Whence come these barbarians?
What shall we call you? So outlandishly

Arrayed in the barbaric luxury
Of robes and crowns, and not in Argive fashion
Nor in Greek? But at this I wonder: how   240
Without a herald, without a guide, without patron,
You have yet dared to come, without trembling.
The suppliant olive branch before these gods
You've placed (it is custom); but Greece no more
Than that will guess: in other things I could
Conjecture only, unless your voice will guide.

Chorus
You did not lie about our dress. But to whom
Do I speak? an Argive citizen, or a herald
With his sacred staff, or the city's head?

King
Answer me with trust: I am Pelasgus,
Founder of this land, and son of Palaechthon   250
Earth-born. Pelasgians bear my royal name,
And reap the fruits of this earth. I rule the lands
In which the pure Strymon turns, where the sun
Sinks in the west, and limits the Perrhaebi,
Beyond the Pindus, near the Paeoni
And the mountain Dodona: oceans bound my rule:
I lord it over all within that frame.
It is called Apia, after a surgeon   260
Of ancient times, the prophet Apis, son
To Apollo, who from Naupactus once did come,
And cleansed this land of deadly, monstrous
Serpents, that the earth, soaked in old
Curses of blood, had sprung and smeared in wrath.
His remedies and herbs did work a cure
For Argos, where his pay's remembrance found
In litanies. There are my testaments.   270
And now you must tell your own ancestry.
The city, though, 's impatient with long speeches.

Chorus
Brief and clear is my tale: by race we claim

Argos, the offspring of a fruitful cow.
I'll tell you how close truth clings to it.

King
You speak beyond my credence, strangers, claiming
Argive birth: more like Libyans you seem
Than like to women native here; or the Nile may foster   280
Such a likeness; or the images
Of Cyprus, carved by native craftsmen;
And of the camel-backed nomads I've heard,
Neighbors to the Ethiopian;
I should have thought you were the unwed
Barbarous Amazons, were you armed with bows.
But, once instructed, I should more fully know
How your birth and ancestry is Argive.   290

Chorus
Wasn't Io once in Argos charged
With Hera's temple?

King
                        Io was, the tale
Is prevalent.

Chorus
                        And wasn't Zeus to a mortal
Joined?

King
            Which was from Hera unconcealed.

Chorus
How end these royal jealousies?

King
                                A goddess
Changed a woman to a cow.

Chorus
                                And Zeus,   300
Did he approach the hornèd cow?

15

King

Zeus

Became a bull, they say.

Chorus

How then did Hera answer?

King

She placed on her a guard, all-seeing.

Chorus

Who?

King

Argos, a son of Earth, whom Hermes slew.

Chorus

But what did Hera appoint for ill-omened Io?

King

A gnatlike goad it was, or driving sting.

Chorus

That the Nile-dwellers call the gadfly.

King

That drove her from Argos.

Chorus

It confirms my tale. 310

King

And so to Canobus and to Memphis she came.

Chorus

Where Zeus by touch begot a son.

King

Who claims to be the calf of Zeus?

Chorus

Epaphus,

Truly named Caress.

King

And who from him?

Chorus

Libya, reaping the greatest name.

King

And then?

Chorus

Belus of two sons, my father's father.

King

Tell me his name.

Chorus

Danaus, whose brother   320
Fathered fifty sons.

King

Disclose his name
Ungrudgingly.

Chorus

Egyptus. Now knowing my ancient
Lineage, might you succor an Argive band.

King

You seem to share of old this land: but how
Did you bring yourself to leave your father's
Home? What fortune did swoop upon you?

Chorus

Lord Pelasgus, shifting are the ills of men.
Nowhere is trouble seen of the same wing.
Who wished for this unexpected flight,
To land at Argos, formerly natives here,   330
Cowering in hate of the marriage bed?

King

Why have you come to these assembled gods?
Why do you hold the fresh white olive branch?

Chorus
To be no household-slave to Egyptus' sons.

King
By hatred or by law? ... (*Some verses are missing.*)

Chorus
                 Who buys a master
From kin? ... (*Some verses are missing.*)

King
        So greater grows the strength of mortals.

Chorus
To desert those distressed is easy.

King
                    How
With piety could I act?

Chorus
             Deny the demand   340
Of Egyptus' sons.

King
          But hard's *your* demand to wage
A new war.

Chorus
       But justice protects her allies.

King
If only she shared from the start.

Chorus
Respect the ship of state thus crowned.

King
I shudder before these shaded altars.

Chorus
Yet hard is the wrath of Zeus the protector.
Son of Palaechthon,
Listen to me with a caring heart,

Lord of Pelasgians.
Protector, behold an exile surrounded:
A calf, wolf-pursued, on steep rocks,   350
Confides in the herdsman's strength,
And bleats her pains.—

King

I see this crowd of gods assenting, each
Shadowed by the fresh-cut olive branch.
Yet may this friendship conceal no doom,
Nor strife for us arise in unexpected
And unpremeditated ways.

Chorus

Daughter of Zeus,
Master of lots, may behold a flight   360
Innocent, Themis!
And thou from the younger, ancient in wisdom,
Learn, . . .
Respecting the suppliant,
A holy man.=

King

You are not suppliants at my own hearth.
If the city stains the commonweal,
In common let the people work a cure.
But I would make no promises until
I share with all the citizens.

Chorus

You are, yes, the city, the people,   370
A prince is not judged.
The land, the hearth, the altar you rule
With the single vote and scepter;
Enthroned you command,
And fill every need.
Of pollution be watchful.—

King

Pollution on my enemies! Without

Harm I cannot aid you; nor is it sensible
To despise these your earnest prayers.
I am at a loss, and fearful is my heart,
To act or not to act and choose success.   380

Chorus

Regard him, above, the protector,
A watchdog of men
Distressed who sit at neighboring hearths,
But obtain no lawful justice.
Yet anger of Zeus
The Suppliant remains,
Who is charmed by no pity.=

King

If Egyptus' sons rule you by customs
Native to your city, claiming nearest
Of kin, who would wish in that to oppose them?
According to laws at home you must plead,   390
How over you they lack authority.

Chorus

Yet subject to men would I never be!
I plot my course under the stars,
An escape from a heartless marriage.
Take as an ally justice.
Choose the side of the gods.—

King

The choice is not easy: choose me not as judge.
I said before that never would I act
Alone, apart from the people, though I am ruler;
So never may people say, if evil comes,   400
"Respecting aliens the city you destroyed."

Chorus

Both sides he surveys, of related blood
Zeus is, impartial his scales,
To the evil and lawful weighs out

The holy and unjust fairly.
Why fear to act justly?=

King

We need profound, preserving care, that plunges
Like a diver deep in troubled seas,
Keen and unblurred his eye, to make the end
Without disaster for us and for the city;   410
That neither strife may bring reprisals, nor,
If we should give you back, seated thus
On seats of gods, we settle the god, destructive
Alastor, in this land, who even in Hades
Never frees the dead. Seem we not
To need preserving counsel?

Chorus

Take care and be,
Justly, the pious protector,
Exile betray not,   420
Exile pursued by,
Cast out by, the godless.—

See me not seized,
From seat of gods to be seized,
O lord with full power.
Know the pride of men,
Beware of God's anger.=

Bear not to see
A suppliant by force   430
Led from these statues,
Seized by my garments,
Like a horse by the bridle.—

Do what you will,
Thy house remains to pay,
Fined in thy children:
Justice is equal.
Mark the justice of Zeus.=

King
I have pondered, and here I'm run aground:
'Gainst you or them necessity is strained   440
For mighty war, as fastly drawn as ships
Held by the windlass: yet anchorage is never
Free from pain. When wealth is sacked and homes
Are pillaged, Zeus yet another fortune may bestow;
Or when the tongue has failed, a healing word
May spread a counter-balm: but if consanguine
Blood is to stay unshed, we must sacrifice
To slaughter many kine to many gods,   450
A cure of grief. I am spent by this dispute:
I wish an ignorance more than art of ill:
Against my judgment may it turn out well.

Chorus
But hear the end of my reverent prayers.

King
Well?

Chorus
    Clasps and belts and bands I have.

King
They are doubtless proper for women.

Chorus
                   Here, you know,
Are fine devices.

King
          Tell me.   460

Chorus
               Unless you promise—

King
What would your bands accomplish?

Chorus
Statues with new tablets to adorn.

King

                            Speak simply.

Chorus
From these gods to hang.

King

                      A whip to the heart.

Chorus
Now you understand, for eyes I gave you.

King
Alas! everywhere I'm gripped in strangle holds,
And like a swollen river evils flood:
Embarked on a sea of doom, uncrossed, abysmal,   470
Nowhere is anchorage. If I leave
This debt unpaid, you've warned of pollution
That shall strike unerringly; but if
I stand before these walls, and bring the battle
To the very end against Egyptus'
Sons, wouldn't that become a bitter waste—
Men to bleed the earth for women's sake?
But yet the wrath of Zeus the Suppliant—
The height of mortal fear—must be respected.
Now then, agèd father of these maidens,   480
Gather those wreaths in your arms; and at other
Altars of the native gods replace them:
Then no one of the native people, who delight
In blame, by seeing proof of your arrival,
Could reproach me; and pity they may feel
For you, and hate those men's arrogance.
May the people be gracious! Everyone,
To those weaker than themselves, is kind.

Danaus
To have found a stranger, reverent and kind,   490
We highly prize. And now, let native guides,
To grant me safety as I go, escort me

To the temple altars: nature made
My shape unlike to yours, even as the Nile
And the Inachus bear no resemblance
In their nurture. Beware lest rashness burgeon
Into fear: ignorance has often killed
A friend.

King

      Attend: the stranger speaks well.   500
Guide him to the civil altars, the seats
Of gods; and say no more than this to whom
You meet: "To the gods' hearth we bring a sailor."

          (Exit Danaus, attended.)

Chorus

Him you instructed, and he is gone; but I,
How shall I act? What sign of confidence
Is yours to give me?

King

          Leave your wreaths here,
A sign of grief.

Chorus

      And here I leave them by your
Command.

King

     Toward that grove now turn.

Chorus

             But how
Would a public grove protect me?

King

           Never   510
To rape of birds shall we expose you.

Chorus

But to them more hateful than heartless snakes?

King
Propitiated, speak auspiciously.

Chorus
You know how fear does fret impatiently?

King
Excessive fear is always powerless.

Chorus
Soothe then my heart in word and deed.

King
Your father will not long desert you; and I,
Assembling all the native people, shall
Make the commons well disposed, and teach
Your father all that he must say.
Now remain here, and beseech the native   520
Gods with your prayers to bring what you desire.
I shall go arranging all: may Persuasion
And Fortune attend me!

                              (*Exit King.*)

Chorus
Lord of Lords most bless'd,
Most perfect strength of bless'd,
Happy Zeus obey
And let it be:
Remove the pride of men,
Pride well hated;
And cast in a purpled sea
The black-benched doom.—   530

Look upon our race
Ancient of ancestor loved,
Change to a happy tale
Favoring us:
Remember many things,
You touched Io.
We claim a descent from Zeus,
And birth from this land.=

To my mother's ancient track I turned,
In a rich pasture eating flowers
She was seen, whence Io   540
By gadfly raged
Distraught escaped;
Passing many races,
Cutting in two the land,
The raging strait defined;—

Through lands of Asia fast she went,
And across Phrygia grazing sheep;
And the city of Teuthras passing,
And Lydian vales,   550
Cilician hills,
Race Pamphylian hurried
Through ever-flowing streams,
And land of Aphrodite.=

She came by dart distressed
Of a cowherd winged
To rich groves of Zeus,
A pasture fed by snow and attacked
By Typhon's rage,   560
The Nile-waters by disease untouched;
Herself crazed,
With grief, stinging pains,
Bacchant of Hera.—

And men who then lived there
At her strangeness trembled,
With pale fear at heart,
Beheld a creature vexed, half-breed,
In part a cow,
And woman in turn, a monster marveled at.   570
Who then charmed
The wretch wandering-far
Furious Io?=

Of endless sovereignty
Lord Zeus charmed,

26

By strength gentle of Zeus
And divine breaths
Was she cured, weeping
Her grievous shame,
Bearing the burden of Zeus,   580
Told without falsehood,
She bore a blameless child,—

Through great time bless'd;
All earth shouts,
"Of Zeus fruitful in truth
This race: who else
Would cure her of sly
Diseases of Hera?"
There is the working of Zeus,
Here is Epaphus' race:
Of both the truth is spoken.=

Whom beside him   590
More justly would I call?
Father our gardener, worker, and lord,
A craftsman aged in wisdom,
Propitious the wind is of Zeus.—

Stronger none rule,
Beneath no one enthroned,
Seated above he respects none below.
His deeds are quick as words,
He hastens what counsel decrees.=

(Enter Danaus.)

Danaus
Take heart, my children, well are cast the people's   600
Final vote.

Chorus
      O hail, my envoy, my dearest
Herald. Tell us what end's been authorized?
And where the populace, by show of hands,
Has thrown its weight.

Danaus

The Argives have decreed
Not doubtfully, so as to change my aging
Heart to youth again; so bristled thick
The air with hands, resolving thus the law:
Free we are to settle here, subject
Neither to seizure nor reprisal, claimed   610
Neither by citizen nor foreigner.
But if they turn to force, whoever rich
In lands refuses succor, shall be stripped
Of offices and banished publicly.
The king persuaded, prophesying Zeus
The Suppliant would fatten rich his wrath
To feed insatiate suffering,
And show itself as twin defilements,   620
In and outside the city. Hearing this,
The Argives, not even summoned, voted all.
They heard, and easily were convinced by supple
Rhetoric; but Zeus still crowned the end.

Chorus

Come then, let us offer
For the Argives good prayers,
A return for good things.
And may Zeus Stranger behold
From the mouth of a stranger
Offerings in true frankness,
A perfect end for all things.

And now Zeus-born gods   630
Might you hear our prayers,
When libations we pour:
Never slain by fire
This Pelasgian land,
Never wanton War
Found a danceless cry,
Harvesting mortals
In a changed harvest;
    For compassion they showed us,

28

And voted with kindness,   640
Respecting Zeus's suppliants,
This wretched flock of sheep.—

Nor cast they their votes
On the side of men
By dishonoring us;
Watching Zeus Avenger
(Like a spy he sees)
Who is hard to fight:
Who desires his home
Stained in its rafters?   650
For he heavily presses.
    The suppliants of Zeus sacred,
    Related blood, they respected.
    Then to gods shall they be pleasing
    With altars scoured clean.=

So out of shadowed lips let fly
Honorable prayers:
Never a plague
Empty the city,   660
Strife never bleed
With native dead the land.
    Flower of youth may it ripen unplucked,
    And partner of Aphrodite, War,
    May he cut not their bloom.—

And laden altars, welcoming,
Set them ablaze.
Well would be ruled
Cities respecting   670
Zeus above all,
Who guides by ancient law.
    Other protectors we pray to be born
    For always, and Hecate-Artemis
    Birth by women protect.=

Let no murderous plague
Come upon the city destroying,   680

29

Without the dance, without lute
Father of tears Ares arming,
And the intestine war's shout.
　May the bitter swarms of ill
　Far from the people sit;
　May the Lycian Apollo
　To all the youth be kind.—

And may Zeus to perfection
Bring the fruit of each season;　　　　　　　　　690
And many young in the fields
Pasturing cattle beget:
May they obtain from gods all.
　May the pious songs be sung
　At altars by minstrels;
　May the lyre-loving voices
　From holy lips arise.=

May the people who strengthen the city
Protect its dignity well;
Whose rule's providential in common counsel;　　700
And before arming Ares,
To strangers without grief
May they grant justice.—

May the gods who possess the city
Be honored by citizens well
With sacrificial laurel, ancestral.
For respect of one's parents
Is third among laws
Written by Justice.=

Danaus

Thank you, dear children, for these modest prayers;　710
But from your father tremble not to hear
New intelligence. From this outpost,
Protector of suppliants, I spy that ship;
Clearly it shows; nor do I fail to mark
How its sails are trimmed and sides made fast,

And how her bow does seek the way with painted
Eye; and the ship, obedient, hears all too well
Her tiller's governance. And the men on board
I see, black in limb, their clothes white linen.
All the other ships and allied force   720
I see; but under land the lead, its sail
Now furling, rows with timèd beat. And you
Must, quietly and temperately facing
The event, ignore none of these gods.
And I, with advocates, shall come. Perhaps
An envoy or a herald comes, desiring
To lead you away as reprisals.
But nothing shall happen. Never fear him.
Still it is better, if we are slow,   730
That refuge to remember. Take heart.
Surely in time the day shall come when all
Who had dishonored the gods shall pay.

Chorus
Father, I fear, as swift ships come;
No length of time does stand between us.
    Terror holds me, excessive fear,
    If flights of wandering profit not.
    Father, I am spent by fear.—

Danaus
As final was the Argive vote, my daughters,
Take heart: they shall fight for you, I know.   740

Chorus
Mad is the race Egyptian, cursed,
In war unsated: I speak what you know.
    Dark ships they have, and strongly built;
    They sailed and so succeed in anger
    With an army large and dark.=

Danaus
But here many shall they find, whose limbs
The sun's made lean in noonday heat.

31

Chorus

Leave us not behind, alone, father! I pray.
Women are nothing alone; no Ares is in them.
   Deadly purposed and crafty minds   750
   With impure hearts, just as ravens,
   They heed no altar.—

Danaus

Well that would aid us, my daughters,
If to the gods, as to you, they are hateful.

Chorus

They feared not these tridents, no awe of gods;
Their hands they shall not keep from me, father.
   Arrogant with unholy rage,
   Gluttonous, dog-hearted, obeying
   In nothing the gods. =

Danaus

A fable tells that wolves possess more strength   760
Than dogs, and reeds cannot conquer wheat.

Chorus

We must guard ourselves against the rage
Of wanton men, monstrous and profane.

Danaus

The reefing of a sail is never swift,
Nor is the anchoring, with ropes to be secured;
And even safe at anchorage the helmsman
Lacks courage, and mostly when come to harborless
Shores, and the sun has sneaked away to night,
It breeds in prudent pilots pain as sharp   770
As birth itself; nor would a host find landing
Easy, before each ship takes courage in
Her moorings. But you, fearful at heart, take heed
Of the gods, while I, bringing aid, shall return
To defend you: an agèd messenger the city
Cannot blame, youthful in eloquence.

                      (Exit Danaus.)

Chorus

O mountainous land, justly respected,
What shall befall us? Where shall we flee,
If in Apian lands some dark abyss somewhere?
Black smoke might I be
Bordering clouds of Zeus;   780
Invisible completely
As unseen dust might I die.—

My heart without fright would no longer be;
Darkness flutters in my heart.
I am seized by his warnings: I am spent by fear.
And willing would I be
Fated to die hanging,
Before that man should touch me: 790
May Hades rule me before!=

Where might there be a throne of air?
Against it wet clouds become snow?
Or smooth, steep, lonely,
Overhanging, distant,
Vulture-haunted rocks,
Witnessing my fall,
Before by force meet
A heart-rending marriage?—

Prey then for dogs and native birds,   800
A feast I shall not refuse them.
For death grants freedom
From lámentable ills.
Let that fate before
My marriage-bed come.
But where is still means
To free us from marriage?=

Shriek and shout a cry to heaven,
Perfect prayers to the gods,
To me relief and fulfilment;   810
And father, seeing the battle,
Behold with just eyes

33

Violence unkindly.
Respect your suppliants,
Protector, omnipotent Zeus!—

Proud and heartless Egyptians—
Men pursuing an exile,
Intent on capturing me,
With shouts many and wanton.   820
But you completely,
Zeus, hold the beam of
The balance. What without you
Is brought to completion for men?=

*(Enter Herald of Egyptians, attended.)**

Cry! O woe! Alas!
Here, this ravisher from the ship!
Before that, ravisher, would you die!
I see this beginning of my woes.   830
Alas! O woe! Escape!
Stern-hearted in insolence,
Hard to bear on land, at sea,
Lord of the land, protect us!

Herald
Hurry!
Hasten to the boats
Fast as you are able.
Lest torn and pricked,
Pricked and scratched you'll be,
Bloody and bloodstained,   840
Your heads cut off!
Hurry, hasten, curses! curses! to the boats!

Chorus
On the flowing salt-path
With your masterful pride
With your bolted ship
Would you had died!

---

* The Herald sometimes speaks in "broken Greek."

34

Herald

Cease your cries. Leave your seats. 850
Go to the ships. You without honor,
You without city, I cannot respect.—

Chorus

Never fruitful water
Might I see again, whence
Grows the living root—
Murder!—and blooms.

Herald

I shall lead—I am brave—
Down to the ship, up on the ladder. 860
Willing, unwilling, you shall go.=

Chorus

Oh, alas, woe.
Oh, would that you had helpless died
By the sea-washed grove
Wandering at Sarpedon's tomb,
Piled up with sand 870
Among wet breezes.

Herald

Shriek and shout and call the gods.
You shall not jump the Egyptian ship.
Bewail and shout and mourn with sorrow.—

Chorus

Oh, alas, woe.
Outrage! when you howl off-shore,
With your boasts overflow;
Whom the great Nile might behold
Raging in your pride, 880
And drown your violence.

Herald

Board the swift boat at once!
Let no one falter: I'll have no awe
Of precious curls when I shall drag you.=

35

Chorus
Alas, father, to the sea he leads me;
Like a spider, step by step,
A dream, a black dream,
Cry, O woe, cry!
Earth, Mother Earth,   890
Avert his fearful cry.
O son, son of Earth, O Zeus.

Herald
I do not fear these gods before me: they
Did not nurse me, their nursing did not age me.—

Chorus
A two-footed serpent quivers near,
Like a viper, bites my foot,
A poisonous thing.
Cry, O woe, cry!
Earth, Mother Earth,
Avert his fearful cry.   900
O son, son of Earth, O Zeus.

Herald
Your finery I shall not pity, if
None will go to the ship resignedly.=

Chorus
We perish, lord, we suffer pain!

Herald
O many lords, Egyptus' sons, you soon
Will see—take heart!—and blame no anarchy!

Chorus
O first commanders, undone am I!

Herald
As you're not hasty to heed my words,
It seems I'll have to drag you by the hair.   910

(*Enter the King, attended.*)

King
You there! What is done? By what insolence
Dare you insult this land of Pelasgian men?
Think you you have come to a woman's land? You are
Barbarians, and you trifle insolently
With Greeks, and, off the mark in everything,
In nothing upright stand.

Herald
                              How did I err?
What do I do without justice?

King
                              You know
Not how to be a stranger.

Herald
                              Though finding what I lost?

King
To what patron did you speak?

Herald
                              To Hermes the Searcher,   920
The greatest patron.

King
                              You speak of gods but have
No reverence.

Herald
                 The Nile deities I revere.

King
And these gods are nothing?

Herald
                              I'll lead them away,
If no one robs me.

King
                 You shall regret it,
If you touch them.

37

Herald
> You speak unkindly to strangers.

King
The thieves of gods I shall not befriend.

Herald
I shall tell Egyptus' sons.

King
What's that to me that I should yield my flock?

Herald
But if I knew, more clearly could I tell—   930
A herald should report exactly each
Particular. What shall I say? Who's he
That robs me of these cousins? Yet Ares gives
His verdict without witnesses, nor in the grip
Of silver quits his suit, but first many
Are thrown and kick off life.

King
> Why must you tell a name?
You and your shipmates will know soon enough;
Though, were these willing, with good will of heart,
You could lead them away, if pious speech   940
Persuaded them: thus unanimous the vote
Decreed, never to surrender them to force.
Joined, doweled, and bolted stays this law,
That neither scratched on tablets, nor book-sealed,
You hear announced by the tongue of freedom's voice.
Now get out of my sight!

Herald
> We seem to wage new wars.   950
May victory and conquest fall to men!

King
And men is what you'll find here, who don't
Guzzle a brew of barley-beer!

> *(Exit Herald.)*

Now all of you, attended by your maids,
Take heart and go to the well-protected city,
Locked by towers in dense array. And many
Homes there are of public property, and I
Am also housed with a lavish hand; there you may
With many others live; or if it pleases   960
More, you may live alone. Of these the best
And most agreeable choose. Myself and all
The citizens protect you, whose voted will
Is now fulfilled. Why wait for those with more
Authority?

Chorus
In return for good things,
May good things teem,
Best of Pelasgians!
Kindly escort my father here,
Danaus, prudent, brave and wise.   970
His is the counsel where to dwell,
Kindly disposed the place with good
Fame and repute among the people:
Everyone's quick to blame the alien.
May it be for the best!

(*Exit King. Enter Danaus, attended.*)

Danaus
My children, to Argives it is meet to pour   980
Libations, pray and sacrifice as to gods
Olympian, who unhesitant preserved us.
What had been done, for native friends kindly,
Bitterly against your cousins, they heard;
And gave these armed attendants as a meed
Of honor, that no spear-wielded fate be mine
In dying, lest I burden on the land
An ever-living grief. You must be grateful
Even more than I for what I have obtained.   990
Above my other counsels cut this wisdom:
Time becomes the touchstone of the alien,

39

Who bears the brunt of every evil tongue,
The easy targe of calumny. I beg
You not to bring me shame, you who have
That bloom which draws men's eyes: there is no
    simple
Guard for fruit most delicate, that beasts
And men, both winged and footed, ravage: 1000
So Venus heralds harvests lush with love;
And all, at the sleek comeliness of maidens,
Do shoot enchanted arrows from their eyes,
Overcome by desire. Let no shame for us,
But pleasure for our enemies, be done,
For which, in great toil, great seas were ploughed.
We have the choice (mere luck) of living either
With Pelasgus, or at the city's cost.   1010
Only regard this command of your father:
Honor modesty more than your life.

Chorus
All else may gods Olympian bless; but, father,
Be not anxious for our summer's blush,
For, lest the gods deliberate anew,
We'll hold to the course our past intent has set.

Chorus A (of maidens)
Come now to the city,
Praising blessèd lord gods,
Who shelter the city
And about the Erasinus dwell.   1020
Take up and accompany,
Servants, the song, and praise
For the city, no longer the Nile,
Respect with your psalms,—

But streams, that with quiet
Through the land fulness pour,
And gladden this earth with
Waters brilliant and rich.   1030
May Artemis sacred see,

Pitying us: by force
Of Aphrodite no marriage come,
A prize for the hated.=

Chorus B (of servants)
But careless not of Cypris this gracious song:
With power equal to Hera nearest to Zeus,
Honored the goddess sly-intent
In rites sacred and solemn;
Which share with a fond mother
Desire and, to whom no denial,   1040
Persuasion; and Aphrodite
A province to Concord bestowed,
And Eros whispering wanton.—

But bitter winds, and harsh and evil grief,
And battles bloody and deadly I fear before.
How did they sail so easily
In swift-wingèd pursuit?
Whatever is doomed becomes.
Infinite the mind is of Zeus,
Who cannot be bypassed.   1050
To many a woman before
Has marriage come as an ending.=

Chorus A
May great Zeus ward off
An Egyptian marriage for me.

Chorus B
That would be best.

Chorus A
Would you charm the intractable?

Chorus B
But the future you know not.—

Chorus A
But Zeus's mind profound,
How am I to plumb?

Chorus B
Pray for the mean.   1060

Chorus A
What limit do you teach me now?

Chorus B
Ask the gods nothing excessive.=

Chorus
Lord Zeus may he deprive us
Of an ill marriage
And a bad husband,
As Io was released from ill,
Protected by a healing hand,
Kind might did cure her.—

And strength may he assign us.
I am content if ill   1070
Is one-third my lot,
And justly, with my prayers,
Beside the saving arts of god,
To follow justice.=

                                    (Exeunt omnes.)

THE PERSIANS

Translated by S. G. Benardete

freedom and slavery. Here are the Persians, having stacked an unjust war and suffering a deserved defeat, presenting not as criminals but rather as great and noble, dying deaths that

INTRODUCTION TO
THE PERSIANS

The Persians was produced at Athens in 472 B.C., eight years
after the naval battle at Salamis, which the play celebrates.
We learn from its Argument that it was modeled on a lost
play, *The Phoenissae* of Phrynichus, but that Phrynichus
had announced at once the defeat of Xerxes, whereas
Aeschylus presents a chorus of old men who voice their
hopes and fears, by themselves and with Xerxes' mother,
before the news of the defeat comes. This delay of course
makes the Persians' defeat so much the greater, as it
heightens the magnificence of their doom. The Queen then
invokes her dead husband Darius (at whose tomb the scene
is laid), who had led an unsuccessful expedition against
Greece ten years before. He consoles the Queen and Chorus
but predicts another disaster at Plataea (479 B.C.). Soon
afterward, Xerxes, his garments torn, returns alone, and he
and the Chorus conclude the play with a lament.

The Persians is unique in several ways. It is the only
extant Greek tragedy that is not mythical but based on a
contemporary event. The daring of such a presentation is
easy to imagine. To show sympathetically, *sine ira et studio*,
on the stage at Athens the defeat of her deadliest enemy
testifies to the humanity of Aeschylus and the Athenians. No
other tragedian we know of, of any country at any time, has
ever dared to go so far in sympathizing with his country's
foe. It is the more remarkable when we consider that
Aeschylus himself and almost all of his audience fought at
Salamis or Plataea and that the war, moreover, was between
freedom and slavery. Here are the Persians, having started
an unjust war and suffering a deserved defeat, presented not
as criminals but rather as great and noble, dying deaths that

45

are to be as much pitied as the deaths of Athenians. To praise the Athenians at Athens, Socrates remarks, or the Spartans at Sparta is not very difficult; but to praise the Athenians at Sparta or the Spartans at Athens demands great rhetorical skill; and for Aeschylus to praise before their conquerors the Persians, the enemies of all Greece, is without precedent and without imitation.

Although *The Persians* is historical in substance, Aeschylus deliberately introduced what the entire audience must have known to be false. He makes up Persian names, very few of which correspond to the generals we know to have been at the battle; his figures for the size of Xerxes' fleet at Salamis are greatly exaggerated; the Persians call upon Greek gods, though everyone knew that their gods were different; the Queen performs a Greek sacrifice at the tomb of Darius; neither the Chorus (except once) nor Darius mention the Persians' defeat at Marathon only ten years before; and perhaps what is most striking, Aeschylus invokes from the past Darius, so that his presence, being both ghostly and real, might transform an ugly reality into a poetic past. By thus changing many details of the real story, Aeschylus removes the Persian War to the realm of myth, where the memory of his audience is prevented from confirming or denying at every point the truth of what he says.

The contemporary is almost perforce untragic, for excessive attention to detail (and the contemporary must be shown accurately) stifles poetry and does not allow the poet to alter his subject; whereas tragedy, being abstracted from the present, is given a free rein, unhampered by what the audience knows to be so, to mold the story to its own demands. Just as verse is an abstraction from prose, reducing it to order, so tragedy abstracts from history and brings necessity out of chance.

If Aeschylus addressed his play specifically to his Athenian countrymen, how can he also speak to us, who are not Athenians, across the reach of time? This certainly must be said. The Persian War was not merely one parochial war among others, in which the issues of right and wrong are ambiguous, as was the case in the Peloponnesian War. The Persian War was a war of liberty versus despotism, and all free men of all times in reading *The Persians* will identify their cause with the cause of the Greeks. In this sense, then, we are Athenians ourselves, and thus our sympathies and understanding become sufficiently enlarged to comprehend the merits of our foes.

Since the doom of the Persians is impressed upon us by the regular meters of the chorus, which convey even to our ears the effect of marching or lament, I have tried, so far as English would allow, to reproduce them in such a way that the reader can "hear" the mood of each song. I hope that, after a little practice on his part, the rhythm will become clear.

CHARACTERS

Chorus of Persian elders

*Queen of Persia, wife of Darius,
    mother of Xerxes*

Persian Herald

Ghost of Darius

Xerxes

THE PERSIANS

SCENE: *In the background the palace of Xerxes at
Sousa, in the center foreground the tomb of
Darius.*

Chorus
Of the Persians gone
To the land of Greece
Here are the trusted:
As protectors of treasure
And of golden thrones
We were chosen by Xerxes—
Emperor and king,
Son of Darius—
In accord with age
Guards of the country.

For the king's return
With his troops of gold
Doom is the omen   10
In my heart convulsed,
As it whines for its master;
For all Asia is gone:
To the city of Persians
Neither a herald nor horseman returns.

And some Agbatana
And some Sousa and
Ancient Kissa leaving,
Both on horse and on ship
And on foot displayed
Legions of battle: 20
Artaphrenes, Megabates,

49

Astaspes, Amistres,
Leaders of Persians, kings,
Who are slaves of the greatest of kings,
Guarding the legions they rush,
And as bowman and knight,
With their temper resolved,
Fearful in aspect,
Dreadful in battle.

And exultant in horses
Artembares, Masistres,
The brave archer Imaeus,
And Pharandakas,
And the driver of horses
Sousthenes.

And others were sent
By the flourishing Nile:
Egyptian-born Sousiscanes,
Pegastagon, great Arsames
Ruler of sacred Memphis;
And Ariomardus
Governing ancient Thebes;
And who dwelling by marshes
Are rowers of ships,
Skilful and countless.

And the Lydians soft
Who inhabit the coast
Follow commanders and kings:
Metrogathes and brave Arkteus,
And golden Sardis send
Many charioteers,
Horses by threes and by fours,
Fearful the sight to behold.

And the neighbors of Tmolus—
They threaten to yoke
In servitude Hellas;
And the Mysian lancers,

Tharybis, Mardon,
Anvils of battle.
And golden Babylon
Pours forth her crowds—
Borne by their ships—
Who in drawing the bow
Rely on their boldness.
And the tribes from all Asia
Who carry the sword
Follow beneath the
Awesome parade of their king.

Thus of the Persian land
Of her men the flower is gone,
Nursed by the earth, and all Asia   60
Laments, consumed by desire;
And parents and wives
Counting the days
Tremble at lengthening time.

The destroyer of cities now,
That kingly army, has gone
Over the strait to the land
On linen-bound pontoons—
Tightly was clamped the way—
Helle of Athamas crossing,   70
Yoking the neck of the sea.—

And the furious leader the herd
Of populous Asia he drives,
Wonderful over the earth,
And admirals stern and rough
Marshals of men he trusts:
Gold his descent from Perseus,
He is the equal of God.=   80

In his eyes lazuli flashing
Like a snake's murderous glances,
With his mariners, warriors, many,
And his Syrian chariot driving,

51

Hard on the glorious spearmen
The archer Ares he leads.—

To the great torrent of heroes
There is none worthily equal,
Who resist, by defenses securèd,
The unconquerable billows of ocean: 90
Persians are never defeated,
The people tempered and brave.=

For divine fate has prevailed since   102
It enjoined Persians to wage wars,
Which destroy towers and ramparts,
And the glad tumult of horsemen,
And cities overthrown.—

When the vast ocean was foaming,
By the winds boisterous whitened,
Then they learned, trusting to cables
And to pontoons which convey men,
To scan the sacred sea.=   113

   Deceitful deception of God—   93
   What mortal man shall avoid it?
   With nimbleness, deftness, and speed,
   Whose leaping foot shall escape it?
   Benign and coaxing at first
   It leads us astray into nets which
   No mortal is able to slip,
   Whose doom we never can flee.   101

Thus sable-clad my heart is torn,
Fearful for those Persian arms,
Lest the city hear, alas!
That reft of men is Sousa;—

And lest the city Kissa shall,
When the crowds of women cry,
Sing antiphonal, alas!   120
And rend their garb of mourning.=

All the horse and infantry
Like a swarm of bees have gone
With the captain of the host,
Who joined the headlands of either land,
Crossing the yoke of the sea.—   130

Beds with longing fill with tears,
Persian wives in softness weep;
Each her armèd furious lord
Dismissed with gentle love and grief,
Left all alone in the yoke.=

But come, Persians,   140
Let us in this ancient palace sit,
And deep and wisely found our thoughts:
How does King Xerxes fare, Darius' son,
How fare his people? Has arrows' hail
Or strength of spear conquered?   150
But lo! she comes,
A light whose splendor equals eyes of gods,
The mother of our king, I kneel.
Now all must address and salute her.

(Enter Queen.)

O most majestic Queen of Persians
In ample folds adorned,
Hail, agèd Xerxes' mother,
Consort of Darius, hail!
Mistress of the god of Persians,
Mother of a god thou art,
Unless the fortune of their arms
Now at last has altered.

Queen

Leaving my gold-clad palace, marriage-
Chamber of Darius, and my own,   160
His queen I'm come. Care quite grates my heart;
I fear, my friends, though not fearful for myself,
Lest great wealth's gallop trip prosperity—

Exalted by Darius and some God—
In its own dust. But, unexpectedly,
That dread has doubled: sums of cowardly
Wealth do court contempt, and indigence
Quenches ambition's flame, even if there's strength.
Though wealth we have unstinted; yet fear
Is for mine eye, Xerxes, whose presence here
I count the palace-eye. So things stand thus.   170
Advise my reason, Persians, old sureties:
All my gains with your counsel lie.

Chorus

O Queen of Persia, be assured that never
Twice hast thou to tell us word or deed,
Which our willing strength can guide; for we
Are loyal, whom thou dost call thy counselors.

Queen

With frequent, constant, and nocturnal dreams
I have lived, as soon as my son, gathering
His host had gone, his will to pillage Greece;
But never a more vivid presence came
Than yesternight's.   180
Two women as an apparition came,
One in Persian robes instructed well,
The other Doric, both in splendor dressed,
Who grand and most magnificent excelled
Us now, their beauty unreproached, spotless;
Sisters they, who casting for their father's land,
She Greece received, she Asia, where to dwell.
Then strife arose between them, or so I dreamed;
And my son, observing this, tries to check   190
And soothe them; he yokes them to a chariot,
Bridles their necks: and one, so arrayed, towers
Proud, her mouth obedient to reins;
But the other stamps, annoyed, and rends apart
Her trappings in her hands; unbridled, seizes
The car and snaps its yoke in two;

My son falls, and his father, pitying,
Stands by his side, but at whose sight Xerxes
Tears his robes. Thus in the night these visions
Dreamed: but when, arisen, I touched the springs'   200
Fair-flowing waters, approached the altar, wishing
To offer sacrifice religiously
To guardian deities, whose rites these are,
Then to Phoebus' hearth I saw an eagle fleeing:
Dumb in dread I stood: a falcon swooped
Upon him, its wings in flight, its claws plucked
At his head: he did no more than cower, hare-like.
Those were my terrors to see, and yours to hear.   210
My son, should he succeed, would be admired;
But if he fails, Persia cannot hold him
To account. Whichever comes, safe returned, sovereign
He shall rule.

Chorus
        Queen mother, excessive fear
Or confidence we do not wish to give thee.
If thy dreams were ominous, approach
The gods with supplications; pray that these
Be unfulfilled, and blessings be fulfilled
For thee, thy son, thy city, and thy friends.
Next thou must libations pour to Earth
And dead; and beg Darius, of whom thou didst dream,   220
Send thee those blessings from the nether world
To light, for thee and for thy son; and hide
In darkness evils contrary, retained
Within the earth. Propitious be thy prayers.
We, prophetic in our spirit, kindly
Counsel thee: all will prosper.

Queen
Ah, loyally have answered the first expounders
Of my dreams. May these blessings ripen!
And all, as you enjoin, I'll sacrifice
To nether gods and friends, as soon as I

55

Return. But one thing more I wish to know: 230
My friends, where is Athens said to be?

Chorus
Far toward the dying flames of sun.

Queen
Yet still my son lusts to track it down?

Chorus
Then all Hellas would be subject to the king.

Queen
So rich in numbers are they?

Chorus
                 So great a host
As dealt to Persians many woes.

Queen
Are bow-plucked shafts their armament?

Chorus
Pikes wielded-close and shielded panoplies.

Queen
What else besides? Have they sufficing wealth? 240

Chorus
Their earth is veined with silver treasuries.

Queen
Who commands them? Who is shepherd of their host?

Chorus
They are slaves to none, nor are they subject.

Queen
But how could they withstand a foreign foe?

Chorus
Enough to vanquish Darius' noble host.

Queen
We mothers dread to calculate—

Chorus

But soon thou'lt know all: a Persian runner comes,
Bearing some fresh report of weal or woe.

(*Enter Herald.*)

Herald

O cities of Asia, O Persian land,
And wealth's great anchorage!
How at a single stroke prosperity's   250
Corrupted, and the flower of Persia falls,
And is gone. Alas! the first herald of woe,
He must disclose entire what befell:
Persians, all the barbarian host is gone.

Chorus

O woe! woeful evil,
Novel and hostile.
Alas! Persians weep
Hearing this woe,—

Herald

How all has been destroyed, and I behold   260
The unexpected light of my return.

Chorus

Oh long seems our aged
Life to us elders,
Alas! hearing woe
Unexpected.=

Herald

And since I was witness, deaf to rumor's tales,
I can indicate what sorrows came.

Chorus

Woe upon woe, in vain
The crowd of arrows, massed,   270
Came on the hostile land.—

Herald
The lifeless rotting corpses glut the shore,
And adjacent fields of Salamis.

Chorus
Woe upon woe, of friends
The sea-dyed corpses whirl
Vagrant on craggèd shores.=

Herald
The bow protected none, but all the host,
Defeated in the naval charge, was lost.

Chorus
Raise a mournful, doleful cry   280
For Persians wretched:
All they made all woe.
Alas! the host destroyed.—

Herald
O most hateful name of Salamis!
O woe! how I mourn recalling Athens.

Chorus
Athens hateful to her foes.
Recall how many
Persians widowed vain,
And mothers losing sons.=

Queen
Long am I silent, alas! struck down
By disasters exceeding speech and question.   290
Yet men perforce god-sent misfortunes must
Endure. Speak, disclose entire what
Befell, quietly, though you grieve.
Who did not die? For whom of the captains
Shall we lament? Whose sceptered death drained his
    ranks
Manless?

58

Herald
> Xerxes lives to behold the light, but—

Queen
O for my palace a greater light,   300
And after blackest night a whiter day.

Herald
Artembares, captain of ten thousand
Horse, was dashed against Silenia's
Rugged shore; and satrap Dadakes,
Spear-struck, did lightly tumble from his ship;
And native-born Tenagon, the bravest
Bactrian, still haunts sea-buffeted
Ajax' isle; and Lilaeus, Arsames,
And Argestes, conquered near the island
Where doves do thrive, beat a stubborn coast;   310
And neighbors of Egyptian Nile-waters,
Adeues, Arkteus, and, third, shielded
Pharnouchus, from a single ship
Were drowned; and Matallus, satrap of Chrysa,
Dying, leader of a thousand horse,
Changed to richest red his thickset flowing
Beard, and dipped his skin in crimson dyes;
And Magian Arabus and Bactrian
Artabes, all aliens in a savage
Country, perished; Amphistreus, who wielded
The much-belaboring spear, and Amistris,   320
Brave Ariomardus, all made Sardis weep;
And Mysian Seisames, Tharybis,
Commander of five times fifty ships,
His race Lyrnaean, fair to look upon
(His fortune was not), dead he lies;
And the leader of Cilicians single-handed
Taxed the enemy with toil, and nobly
Died. So many of the rulers I
Recall, but of the many woes, report
But few.   330

59

Queen
      Alas! I hear the greatest
Of misfortunes, shame of Persians, and shrill
Lament. But tell me, returning to your tale,
What was the number of the Grecian ships,
That thought themselves a match for Persian
Arms in naval combat?

Herald
              Had numbers counted,
The barbarian warships surely would have won;
The Greeks but numbered thirty tens, and ten   340
Apart from these a chosen squadron formed;
But Xerxes, and this I know full well, a thousand
Led; and seven and two hundred ranked
As queens in swiftness. The count stood so.
Seemed we unequal? Some deity destroyed
Our host, who weighing down the balance swung
The beam of fortune. The gods saved the city
Of the Goddess.

Queen
      What? Athens still
Stands unsacked?

Herald
      As long as there are men
The city stands.

Queen
      What was the beginning   350
Of disaster? Tell me. Who began?
The Greeks? My son—exultant in his numbers?

Herald
Either an avenger or a wicked
God, my Lady (whence it came I know not),
Began the whole disaster. From Athenian
Ranks a Greek approached, addressing Xerxes
Thus: "When the gloom of blackest night

Will fall, the Greeks will not remain, but leap
To rowing-bench, and each by secret course
Will save his life." And he your son, upon   360
His hearing this, in ignorance of Greek
Guile and the jealousy of gods,
Harangued his captains publicly: "As soon
As sunlit rays no longer burn the earth,
And darkness sweeps the quarters of the sky,
Rank the swarm of ships in three flotillas,
Guard they the entrances, the straits sea-pound,
And girdle others round Ajax' isle;
But if the Greeks escape their evil doom,   370
Contriving secret flight, all your heads
Will roll. I warrant it." So he spoke
In humored pride: of the God-given future
Nothing he knew. And, having supped, they set
Themselves in order, each heart obedient;
And sailors bound a thong about each oar.
When the glare of sunlight died, and night
Came on, every man was at his oar,
Every man at arms who knew them.
Rank encouraged rank, and long-boats sailed   380
To stations each had been assigned.
All night the captains kept the fleet awake;
And night ran on. No Grecian army set
Secret sail: but when the steeds of day,
White and luminous, began to cross
The sky, a song-like, happy tumult sounded
From the Greeks, and island rocks returned   390
The high-pitched echo. Fear fell among us,
Deceived in hope; for they (and not as if to flee)
A solemn paean chanted, and to battle
Rushed with fervent boldness: trumpets flared,
Putting every Greek aflame. At once
Concordant strokes of oars in dissonance
Slapped the waters' depths: soon we saw
Them all: first the right wing led in order,

Next advanced the whole armada; 400
A great concerted cry we heard: "O Greek
Sons, advance! Free your fathers' land,
Free your sons, your wives, the sanctuaries
Of paternal gods, the sepulchers
Of ancestors. Now the contest's drawn:
All is at stake!" And babel Persian tongues
Rose to meet it: no longer would the action
Loiter. Warships struck their brazen beaks
Together: a Grecian man-of-war began
The charge, a Phoenician ornamented stern 410
Was smashed; another drove against another.
First the floods of Persians held the line,
But when the narrows choked them, and rescue hope-
less,
Smitten by prows, their bronze jaws gaping,
Shattered entire was our fleet of oars.
The Grecian warships, calculating, dashed
Round, and encircled us; ships showed their belly:
No longer could we see the water, charged
With ships' wrecks and men's blood. 420
Corpses glutted beaches and the rocks.
Every warship urged its own anarchic
Rout; and all who survived that expedition,
Like mackerel or some catch of fish,
Were stunned and slaughtered, boned with broken
oars
And splintered wrecks: lamentations, cries
Possessed the open sea, until the black
Eye of evening, closing, hushed them. The sum
Of troubles, even if I should rehearse them
For ten days, I could not exhaust. Rest 430
Content: never in a single day
So great a number died.

Queen
Alas! a sea of troubles breaks in waves
On the Persians and barbarian tribes.

Herald
But what we've told would scarcely balance woes
Untold: misfortune came upon them, which
Swung the beam to weigh them double these.

Queen
But what greater hatred could fortune show?
What misfortune came upon the soldiers,
Swinging the beam of troubles to greater woes?   440

Herald
All the Persians, who were in nature's prime,
Excellent in soul, and nobly bred to grandeur,
Always first in trust, met their death
In infamy, dishonor, and in ugliness.

Queen
Oh, wretched am I, alas! What doom
Destroyed them?

Herald
There is an island fronting Salamis,
Small, scarce an anchorage for ships,
Where the dancer Pan rejoices on the shore;
Whither Xerxes sent those men to kill   450
The shipwrecked enemies who sought the island
As a refuge (easily, he thought,
The Grecian arms would be subdued);
He also bid them rescue friends. He conned
The future ill. For when a God gave Greeks
The glory, that very day, fenced in bronze,
They leaped ashore, and drew the circle tight
At every point: mewed up, we could not turn.
Many rattled to the ground, whom stones
Had felled, and arrows, shot by bowstring,   460
Others killed; and in a final rush,
The end: they hacked, mangled their wretched limbs,
Until the life of all was gone.
Xerxes mourned, beholding the lowest depths
Of woe; who, seated on a height that near

The sea commanded all his host, his robes
Destroying (and his lamentations shrill),
Dispatched his regiments on land: they fled   470
Orderless. Now you may lament their fate,
Added to the others' summed before.

Queen

O hateful deity! how the Persians
You deceived! Bitter was the vengeance
Which my son at famous Athens found:
She could not sate her appetite with those
Whom Marathon had made the Persians lose.
For these my son, exacting as requital
Punishment (or so he thought)
Called on himself so numerous
A train of woes. Tell me, what ships escaped?
Where are they now? Can you clearly tell?

Herald

Who captained the remaining ships set sail   480
Before the wind, fleeing in disorder;
But the army perished in Boeotia: some,
In want of precious water, were racked with thirst,
And some, gasping emptily on air,
Crossed to Phocis, Locria, the Malian
Gulf, where Spercheian waters kindly drench
The plain; and thence Achaea and Thessaly
Received us, wanting: there most died   490
In hunger and in thirst: both we felt.
To Magnesia and Macedonia we came,
The River Axius, the reedy marsh
Of Bolba, the mountain Pangaeon,
And Thrace. There in the night a God
Roused winter out of season: all, who had
Believed the gods were naught, sang their chants,
To earth and sky obeisance made.
When we ceased invoking gods, we tried   500
Waters that had turned to ice:
Whoever started before Apollo's rays

Spread and scattered in the sky, he
Was saved. Soon the brilliant orb of sun,
Its rays aflame, melts the river's midst:
One falls upon the next: happy he whose life
Was first cut short! The rest did make their way   510
But painfully through Thrace: not many fled
To hearth and home. Thus the city of Persians
May lament, regretting the loss of youth.
Truthful I have been, but omit many
Of the woes a God has hurled against
The Persians.

(*Exit Herald.*)

Chorus

O toilsome deity! how heavily
You leaped upon all Persia!

Queen

Alas! woe is me, the host destroyed.
O bright night's spectacle of dreams,
How clearly you foresaw my woe,
And you, my counselors, how poorly judged.   520
But yet, as you counseled thus,
First to the gods I'll offer prayer; and then
To Earth and dead I'll come to offer gifts,
A sacrificial cake. I know I pray
For what is done and gone, but a brighter
Fortune, in time to come, may there be.
And you, worthy of trust, exchange worthy counsel;
My son, should he return before my own
Return, comfort and escort him home:
I fear to woes he'll add more woe.   530

(*Exit Queen.*)

Chorus

O! royal Zeus destroyed
The multitudinous, proud
Host of the Persian men,

And the cities of Sousa
And of Agbatana
Concealed in the darkness of grief.

Many with delicate hands
Rending their veils,
Drenching their breasts,
Swollen with tears,   540
Sharing their woe,
Ladies of Persia
Softly are weeping,
Desiring each
Him to behold
Wedded but lately,
Couches forsaking,
Soft as their coverlets
(Youth was voluptuous),
Their sorrows, insatiate woe.
And I the paean's song recite,
Doom of the gone,
Woe upon woe.

Now all Asia
Desolate, void,
Sighs lament:
Xerxes led,   550
Alas,
Xerxes lost,
O woe,
Xerxes heedless all discharged
With ocean argosies.
Why was Darius so long without harm,
Archery's captain of citizens,
Loved Sousa's lord?—

Armies, navies
Lazuli-eyed,
Linen-winged   560

66

Warships led,
O woe,
Warships rammed destructively
By Grecian arms.
Scarcely escaped was the leader alone
(So we have heard) in the Thracian
Plains, bitter ways.=

They of the first death,
Alas,
Left by necessity,
Woe,
Round by Kychraean shores,   570
Oh,
Moan in your anguish,
Cry to the heavens your grief,
Oh,
Wail long-weeping
Mournful cries.—

Torn in the sea-swirl,
Alas,
Mangled by voiceless,
Woe,
Fish of the unstained sea.
Oh,
Houses deprived grieve,
Sonless, to heavens their grief,   580
Oh,
Elders mourning,
Hear all woe.=

They throughout the Asian land
No longer Persian laws obey,
No longer lordly tribute yield,
Exacted by necessity;
Nor suffer rule as suppliants,
To earth obeisance never make:
Lost is the kingly power.—   590

Nay, no longer is the tongue
Imprisoned kept, but loose are men,
When loose the yoke of power's bound,
To bawl their liberty.
But Ajax' isle, spilled with blood
Its earth, and washed round by sea,
Holds the remains of Persia.=

(*Enter Queen.*)

Queen
My friends, whoever's wise in ways of evil
Knows how, when a flood of evil comes,
Everything we grow to fear; but when   600
A god our voyage gladdens, we believe
Always that fortune's never-changing wind
Will blow. As my eyes behold all things
As fearful visitations of the gods,
So my ears already ring with cureless songs:
Thus consternation terrifies my sense.
Therefore I departed from the palaces,
Alone returning, unaccompanied
By chariots, by pomp and ceremony.
To the father of my son I bring
Propitious offerings, libations   610
For the dead: a milk-sweet draught of sacred kine
Unblemished; and resplendent liquors of the honey-
Working bee, with liquid droplets of a maiden
Stream are mingled; and this elixir
Of an antique vine, whose mother is
The wild fields; and golden-green the fruit
Of fragrant olive trees, always flourishing
Their leafy age; and plaited flowers, children
Of the fecund earth. My friends, recite
Your chants and threnodies; recall
Darius, daemon over these libations   620
To the dead, sepulchral honors, which
I lavish on the nether gods.

68

Chorus
O Queen of the Persians,
To the dark chambers
Libations pour;
While, kindness imploring
Of the gods, the conductors,
We offer prayer:
Ye sacred divinities,
Earth and King Hermes,   630
Conduct him to light
Up from the dead,
Who alone of all mortals,
A remedy knowing,
May show us the end.

Hearest thou, blessèd king
Equal to God,
As I proclaim now
Chantings unpleasant
Barbarous mournful
Clear and diverse?
Miserable sorrows
I shall cry out.
Below dost thou hearken?—

Earth and the other gods   640
Leaders of dead,
Glorious demon
Him let arise thence,
God of the Persians
Sousa his mother;
Send up the man whom
Never surpassed
The Persian land buried.=

Loved is the man, loved his tomb
Hiding his loving ways.
Aedoneus conductor,

69

Would that Aedoneus send 650
Lord Darius alone:—

Never by war wasted his men,
Never infatuate,
Called a God in wisdom,
God in wisdom he was,
Ruled his people well.=

Padshah, ancient Padshah,
Appear on the height of thy tomb,
Raise thy slipper saffron-dyed, 660
Flash the lappets of thy crown:
Father Darius, Oh hither come, woe.—

Hear the recent sorrows,
O master of masters appear.
Stygian gloom doth flit about;
All the youth hath perished now. 670
Father Darius, Oh hither come, woe.=

Oh, alas, Oh!
O much-lamented by his friends in death:
The ships with triple banks of oars are gone. 680

(*The Ghost of Darius rises.*)

Darius
O faithful followers, companions
Of my youth! O Persian counselors!
What burden's burdening the city, which
In lamentation moans, and makes the plains
Tremble? And terrified I saw my wife
Beside my tomb, and graciously received
Her offerings; and you lamented, standing
Near my tomb, with cries of resurrection
Calling piteously. Ascent is not easy.
The chthonic deities more readily
Receive than give; but I, a potentate 690
Among them, came: be quick, that I be un-

Reproached for being late. What recent woe
Upon the Persians weighs?

Chorus
I'm shamed to behold thee,
I'm shamed to address thee,
Who was anciently feared.—

Darius
Since I have risen obeying
Lamentations, lengthen not
Your tale, but speak succinctly,
Recounting all. Lay aside your
Reverence toward me.

Chorus
I tremble to please thee,
I tremble to tell thee
What is loth to be told.= 700

Darius
As an ancient fear obstructs your sense,
You, agèd consort of my marriage,
Noble Queen, cease your weeping; tell me
Clearly: many woes arise by sea, many
Come by land, the longer life is racked.

Queen
O King, exceeding mortal happiness
By happy fate! How, as long as you beheld
The eyes of sun, you spent, how envied! a blessed 710
Life like God's; and now I envy you
Your dying, ere you saw this depth of woe.
Everything, Darius, you will hear
Succinctly: Persia is destroyed.

Darius
How? A lightning-bolt of hunger? Civil
Strife within the city?

Queen

      No, but all
The host's destroyed at Athens.

Darius

        Who among
My sons was general? Tell me.

Queen
Furious Xerxes, who drained the plain manless.

Darius
By foot or warship was his vain attempt?

Queen
By both: a double front of doubled hosts.   720

Darius
But how did so great an army cross the strait?

Queen
Devices, yoking Helle's strait, a path
Afforded.

Darius

   He accomplished this? To close
Great Bosphorus?

Queen

     So it was; some god
Contrived it.

Darius

    Alas! a great divinity
Deceived his sense.

Queen

     The evil end he made
Is present to the eye.

Darius

     What befell them
That you thus lament?

Queen

The naval host,
Destroyed, destroyed the landed host.

Darius
Thus all the people spears destroyed.

Queen
Thus Sousa groans desolate.   730

Darius
Alas! the goodly host! Alas! defenders!
All the Bactrians destroyed, no youth remains.

Darius
O woe! the youth of allies gone.

Queen

Xerxes
Alone with few they say.

Darius

Perished how?
Perished where?

Queen

To the joyous bridge
They came, the yoke of continents.

Darius
He was saved? Can this be true?

Queen
Yes, a clear report without dispute.

Darius
Alas! that prophecy was quick to act!
Zeus hurled against my son its lightning-end,   740
While I expected after many years
The gods would make an end; but when a man's
Willing and eager, god joins in. The spring
Of evil's found: my son in ignorance
Discovered it, by youthful pride; who hoped

To check the sacred waters of the Hellespont
By chains, just as if it were a slave. He smoothed
His way, yoking Neptune's flowing Bosphorus
With hammered shackles. Mortal though he was,
By folly thought to conquer all the gods
And Neptune. Had not my son diseased his sense?   750
I fear my labored wealth will fall the prey
Of conquerors.

Queen

        Wicked men counseled this, furious
Xerxes learned; saying you acquired wealth
By spear, while he, in cowardice, played
The warrior at home, and multiplied
By nothing his ancestral wealth. So often
These wicked men reproached him, until he
Did plot his martial way toward Greece.

Darius

So their great, eternal deed is done!
Never had anyone before made this   760
Sousa so empty and so desolate,
Since Zeus, our Lord, bestowed that honor:
One man to wield his rod's authority
Over all of Asia, rich in flocks.
First was Medus leader of the host;
Next his son fulfilled the office well,
Whose reason was the helmsman to his spirit;
Third was Cyrus, fortunate, whose rule
Brought peace to all: the Lydian people
And the Phrygian he acquired,   770
And marched his might against Ionia:
No god resented him, for he was wise;
And fourth was Cyrus' son, who shamed his country
And ancestral throne; but Artaphrenes
(Aided by his guile) and his friends,
Whose task this was, slew him in his palace.
After him, I, willing, drew the lot
To rule, and often led a mighty host;   780

74

But never did I cast so great a woe
Upon my city. Xerxes, my son, as young
In age as sense, ignored my wisdom. Know
This well, my comrades old as I, all of us
Who held these powers, never wrought so many
Woes.

Chorus

     To what end, my Lord Darius, dost thou
Harp on this? How could we, the Persian
People, fare the best?

Darius

          If you lead
No expedition to the land of Greece,   790
Not even if the Median host be more;
For Grecian soil is their own ally.

Chorus

What dost thou intend by that, "their own ally"?

Darius

It starves to death excessive numbers.

Chorus

But, be sure, we'll raise a well-equipped
And chosen host.

Darius

          But even they, who now
Remain in Greece, shall find no safe return.

Chorus

What? Shall not all the host return
Across the strait of Helle?

Darius

          Few of many,
If the oracles of gods are credited: 800
As we gaze at what has passed, no half
Prophecy succeeds, but either all
Or none. If we credit them, he leaves

75

Behind, his empty hopes persuading, chosen
Numbers of his host, who now are stationed
Where Asopus floods the plain, its rich sap
Kind to Boeotia; here await them
The lowest depths of woe to suffer, payment
For his pride and godless arrogance.
They, invading Greece, felt no awe,
They did not hesitate to plunder images
Of gods, and put temples to the torch;   810
Altars were no more, and statues, like trees,
Were uprooted, torn from their bases
In all confusion. Thus their wickedness
Shall no less make them suffer:
Other woes the future holds in store,
And still the fount of evils is not quenched,
It wells up, and overflows: so great will be
The sacrificial cake of clotted gore
Made at Plataea by Dorian spear.
And corpses, piled up like sand, shall witness,
Mute, even to the century to come,
Before the eyes of men, that never, being
Mortal, ought we cast our thoughts too high.   820
Insolence, once blossoming, bears
Its fruit, a tasseled field of doom, from which
A weeping harvest's reaped, all tears.
Behold the punishment of these! remember
Greece and Athens! lest you disdain
Your present fortune, and lust after more,
Squandering great prosperity.
Zeus is the chastener of overboastful
Minds, a grievous corrector. Therefore advise
Him, admonished by reason, to be wise,   830
And cease his overboastful temper from
Sinning against the gods. And you, aged
Mother of Xerxes, go to the palace;
Gather up rich and brilliant cloths, and go
To meet your son; for he, in grief, has rent
His embroidered robes to shreds. Gently soothe

Him with your words: to yours alone he'll listen.
Now shall I descend to nether gloom.
Elder counselors, farewell, and though
In time of troubles, give daily pleasures   840
To your soul, as wealth cannot benefit
The dead.

(*The Ghost of Darius descends.*)

Chorus
Alas! the woes upon us and the woes
To come have grieved me hearing them.

Queen
O god! how many sorrows move against me!
But one torment has the deepest fang,
Hearing that dishonor folds about my son
Its robes. But I shall go to gather up
Adornments, and try to meet my son.   850
When evils come on those we dearly love,
Never shall we betray them.

(*Exit Queen.*)

Chorus
Oh! alas, Oh! what a great and a good life was ours,
Civilly ordered, as long as the agèd
Ruler of all,
Mild, unconquerable king,
Equal to god,
Darius ruled the land.—

Glorious arms we displayed, and the bulwarks of
  custom
All they did guide. And returning from battle   860
Grief had we none,
Victors, unburdened of all,
Happy and glad,
To home again we came.=

For many the cities he sacked never crossing the
  Halys,
Nor leaving his hearth in a rush:
At the mouth of the River Strymon,
Near Thracian places,
The islands of Achelous;—

Both cities beyond the Aegean, surrounded by towers, 870
Obeyed him our lord, and who round
The broad strait of Helle boasting,
And recessed Propontis,
And gateway of Pontus, Bosphor;=

And the isles along the headland washed by sea 880
Lying close to shore:
Samos and Chios and Lesbos the olive-planted,
Paros and Naxos and Mykonos,
And Tenos the neighbor of Andros.—

And the islands in the midst of sea he ruled:
Ikaros and Lemnos, 890
Rhodus and Knidos and cities of Aphrodite,
Paphos and Solus and Salamis,
Whose founder's the cause of these sorrows.=

Thus the wealthy and populous lands,
The Ionian province, he ruled; 900
And the strength of his helmeted men
Was unwearied, innumerable allies.
But now we bear God-routed fortunes,
Overcome by the blows of the sea.

(*Enter Xerxes alone.*)

Xerxes
Oh, hateful this doom, woe is me,
Wretched alas, without augury. 910
How savagely swooped the deity.
What will befall me? I swoon
Beholding these citizens agèd.

78

Zeus! would that fate had covered me
With the Persians gone!

Chorus
Oh alas, King, for a brave host,
For the great honor of Persian rule,
For the ranks of men whom a god has slain.   920

Nations wail their native sons,
Who by Xerxes stuffed up hell;
Many heroes, Persia's bloom,
Archers, thick array of men,
Myriads have perished.
Woe, O King of noble strength.
Cruel! Cruel! Asia kneels.   930

Xerxes
Here am I, alas, O woe:
To my native and ancestral land
Woe is the evil I've become.

Chorus
Loudly shall I send, for your return,
An evil-omened shout, an evil-practiced cry:
A weeping wail of Persian mourners shall I sing.—

Xerxes
Send a wail of evil sound
Lamenting and grievous: now
Fortune again has changed for me.   940

Chorus
Mourning wail all-weeping shall I send,
In honor of your woes and sea-struck grief:
Again a wailing filled with tears I'll cry.=

Xerxes
Ionian Ares spoiled,
Protected by their ships,
Their partisan in war,   950

79

Reaping gloomy flats of sea
and demon-haunted shores.

Chorus

Oh alas!

Xerxes

Lament and ask for all.

Chorus

But where are the others?
Where is thy retinue,
Like Pharandakas,
Sousas, Pelagon, and Agabatas,
Dotamas, Psammis, Sousiscanes   960
Leaving Agbatana?—

Xerxes

The lost I deserted there,
Who from the ships of Tyre
To Salaminian shore
Vanished and were gone, their corpses
pounding stubborn shores.

Chorus

Oh alas! but where is Pharnouchus
And brave Ariomardus?
Where is Seualkes lord,
Or Lilaeus grand,
Memphis, Tharybis, and Masistres,   970
Artembares and Hystaechmes?
These I ask you about.=

Xerxes

Oh alas, woe,
Who all, beholding ancient, hateful Athens, gasp on
shore,
Woe upon woe, wretched in a single sweep of oar.

Chorus

Did you leave that Persian there,

Your trusted universal eye,   980
Who made his count by myriads,
Batanochus' son Alpistus?

. . . .

Of Sesames, of Megabates,
Great Parthus and Oebares you left behind?
O woe, O woe, O miseries.
You tell of woes on woes.—

Xerxes
Oh alas, woe,   990
The magic wheel of longing for my friends you turn,
    you tell
Me hateful sorrows. Within my frame my heart re-
    sounds, resounds.

Chorus
And for the others still we long:
The leader of ten thousand men
Of Mardia, Xanthes, Angchares,
And Diaexis and Arsamas,
Masters of horsemen,
And Dadakas and Lythimnas,
And Tolmus who never staked his spear.
I see about the moving tents,   1000
I see no followers.=

Xerxes
Gone are the hunters of the pack.

Chorus
Gone, alas, fameless.

Xerxes
Oh alas, woe.

Chorus
Woe, O gods
Who brought these unexpected woes!
How baleful gleams the eye of doom.—

Xerxes
Struck by woes perpetual.

Chorus
Struck by recent—

Xerxes
A recent woe.

1010

Chorus
Woe, alas,
They met the men-of-war without success:
How luckless was the Persians' war.=

Xerxes
Alas, in so vast an army I am struck.

Chorus
What is not lost, thou curse of the Persians?

Xerxes
Behold the remnants of my power.

Chorus
I see, I see.

Xerxes
And this receptacle.

1020

Chorus
What is this that is saved?

Xerxes
A treasure of arrows.

Chorus
How few from so many!

Xerxes
We are reft of protectors.

Chorus
Greeks stand firm in combat.—

Xerxes
Alas, too firm! I scan an unexpected woe.

Chorus
You mean the host, routed and broken?

Xerxes
My garments I rent at my woe.

Chorus
Alas, O woe.   1030

Xerxes
And even more than woe.

Chorus
Double and triple the woe.

Xerxes
Painful to us, but to enemies joy.

Chorus
And docked was our power.

Xerxes
I am stripped of escorters.

Chorus
Sea-dooms stripped us of our friends.=

Xerxes
Weep, weep, weep for the woe, and homeward depart.

Chorus
Alas, O woe, misery.

Xerxes
Shout antiphonal to me.   1040

Chorus
To woebegone woeful gift of woes.

Xerxes
Raising a cry, join together our songs.

Xerxes and Chorus
Alas, O woe, woe, woe upon woe.

Chorus
Hearing this calamity,
Oh! I am pierced.—

Xerxes
Sweep, sweep, sweep with the oar, and groan for my
  sake.

Chorus
I weep, alas, woe is me.

Xerxes
Shout antiphonal to me.

Chorus
My duty is here, O master, lord.

Xerxes
Lift up your voice in lamenting now.   1050

Xerxes and Chorus
Alas, O woe, woe, woe upon woe.

Chorus
Black again the blows are mixed,
Oh, with the groans.=

Xerxes
Beat your breast and cry Mysian songs.

Chorus
Woe upon woe.

Xerxes
Tear your whitened hair tightly clenched.

Chorus
Tightly clenched, plaintive.

Xerxes
Piercing cry.

Chorus
And so I shall.—

Xerxes
Full-fold garments with strength of hand rend.   1060

Chorus
Woe upon woe.

Xerxes
Pluck your hair and pity the host.

Chorus
Tightly clenched, plaintive.

Xerxes
Drench your eyes.

Chorus
And so I weep.=

Xerxes
Shout antiphonal to me.

Chorus
Alas, O woe.

Xerxes
Wretched, homeward depart.

Chorus
O woe, alas.   1070

Xerxes
Through the city lamentation.

Chorus
Lament indeed.

Xerxes
Softly stepping, moan.

Chorus
O Persian land in hardness stepped.

Xerxes
O woe, woe, in triple banks of oars,
O woe, woe, in argosies destroyed.

Chorus
We shall escort thee
With mournful lament.

(*Exeunt omnes.*)

SEVEN
AGAINST THEBES

Translated by David Grene

INTRODUCTION TO
SEVEN AGAINST THEBES

THIS strange, archaic play was produced in 467 B.C. It is
probably the last play of a trilogy written by Aeschylus on
the theme of the Oedipus cycle. It is at once undramatic
and yet, in a paradoxical way, very theatrical. Who can
take seriously a play with almost no action, in which the
main event is the recital of the blazonry on the shields of
the Seven Champions? But a careful reading will reveal the
tremendous effect that the dancing accompaniments would
have made. The effect of the whole is, despite its dis-
advantages for a modern reader, very powerful.

The play is extremely hard to translate. The style is heroic
in the good parts and bombastic in the bad. It is never
simple and luminous. Whereas the same quality of diction in
the elevated parts of the *Prometheus* is always suited to a
majesty of theme comprehensible to a modern reader, the
matter of the *Seven* is remote from the interest of a reader
today, and it needs imagination to conceive of it in the
Greek theater, let alone on the stage as we now know it.

It is perhaps better understood by a modern reader in the
mood in which he would now attend a ritual ceremony, a
church service, or a pageant such as the coronation of an
English monarch. The recital of the devices on the shields,
the matching of the champions, and, in the last part of the
play, the antiphonal keening of the sisters over the dead
bodies of their brothers are all properly traditional ritual.
They were probably filled for the Greek spectator with matter pertinent to his own time. The political relation of Argos,
Thebes, and Athens was then much discussed, and Aeschylus
has undoubtedly used the popular interest in these matters

to render the old story vital for his audience. It may be that the names of the champions had many associations for the mid-fifth-century Greek. Aeschylus has similarly used the general interest in the Areopagus in the years 462–459 B.C. for the pageant drama of the *Oresteia*. Though many of the clues to his employment of this method in the *Seven* are lost to us, we are almost certainly correct in assuming that this is again the course he adopted. The *Seven*, like the *Eumenides*, is the last play of the trilogy, and in both Aeschylus has managed to raise progressively a particular story to the level of a general process of history culminating in a particular historical occurrence known to his contemporaries.

CHARACTERS

Eteocles, son of Oedipus and
  present ruler of Thebes

Antigone
        his sisters
Ismene

Messenger

Chorus of Theban Women

SEVEN AGAINST THEBES

SCENE: *Thebes. The Prince Eteocles confronts a crowd of Thebans.*

Eteocles
You citizens of Cadmus, he must speak home
that in the ship's prow watches the event
and guides the rudder, his eye not drooped in sleep.
For if we win success, the God is the cause
but if—may it not chance so—there is disaster,
throughout the town, voiced by its citizens,
a multitudinous swelling prelude
cries on one name "Eteocles" with groans:
which Zeus defender keep from the city of Cadmus
even as his name implies.
You must help her now—you still something short   10
of your young manhood and you whose time of youth
is gone, your body grown to its full bigness—
each of you to such charge as fits you:
help the city, help the altars of your country's gods;
save their honors from destruction:
help your children, help Earth your Mother.
She reared you, on her kindly surface, crawling
babies, welcomed all the trouble of your nurture,
reared you to live in her, to carry a shield
in her defense, loyally, against such needs as this.   20
Now to this God kindly inclines this day.
For those who have been held in siege so long
the gods grant commonly a favorable fight.
So says the prophet now, bird shepherding
with skill unlying, ears and mind and fire
tending the oracular birds.

The master of these prophecies declares
enemy's night council framed a plot
for the greatest Achaean assault upon us.
All to the battlements, to the gates of the towers!　　30
Haste, in full armor, man the breastworks:
stand on the scaffolding and at the exit gates
be firm, abide, your hearts confident:
fear not that mighty mob of foreigners.
God will dispose all well:
I have sent scouts and spies upon their host:
they will not—well I know it—make the journey
vainly, and by their information
I shall be armed against enemy's stratagems.

Messenger
Eteocles, great prince of the Cadmaeans,
I come bringing a clear word from the army　　40
of matters there: I myself too
have seen the things I speak of.
There were seven men, fierce regiment commanders,
who cut bulls' throats into an iron-rimmed
shield, and with hands touched the bulls' blood,
taking their oaths by Ares and Enyo,
by the bloodthirsty God of Battle Rout
either to lay your city level
with the ground, sacked, or by their death to make
a bloody paste of this same soil of yours.
Remembrances of themselves for parents at home
their hands have hung upon Adrastus' chariot:　　50
their tears ran down,
but never a word of pity was in their mouths.
Their spirits were hard as iron and ablaze
breathed courage: war looked through their lion-eyes.
You will not wait long for confirmation
of this my news: I left them casting lots
how each should lead his regiment against your
　　gates.
Wherefore the choicest men within your city

set at the entrance gates: set them quickly
for near already the armed host of Argives
comes in a cloud of dust, flecks of white,   60
panted from horses' lungs, staining the ground.
You, like the skilful captain of a ship
barricade your town before the blast of Ares
strikes it in storm: already bellows
the armed land wave. Take quickest opportunity
for all these things and I for the rest
will keep my eye, a trusty day watcher.
Thanks to my clear reports you shall know whatever
happens within the gates, and come to no harm.

Eteocles

O Zeus and Earth and gods that guard the city
My father's Curse, mighty evil spirit,   70
do not root out this city of mine, do not
give her to ruin and destruction, do not
give her to capture nor her homes and hearths.
This is a town that speaks with a Greek tongue.
City and land of the Cadmaeans are free:
do not bind her in slavish yoke; be her protector.
I think I speak for everybody's good,
for a city prosperous honors the gods.

Chorus

My sorrows are great and fearful: I cry aloud:
the army has left the camp and is gone.
Look at the forward rushing river, the great tide of
      horsemen!   80
I see a cloud of dust, sky high, and am convinced;
a messenger clear and unlying, though voiceless.

Treading feet on the earth of my country,
trampling hoofs, the sound of these draws near.

(Shout is heard.)

It floats, it rings
like a resistless mountain waterfall.

O gods, O goddesses, the trouble raised!
Turn it aside!

(Shouts.)

Over the walls they spring
the Horse of the White Shield
well equipped, hastening upon our city.   90

Who will protect us? Who will be our champion
of gods or goddesses?
Shall I kneel at the images of the gods?
O Blessed Ones, throned in peace,
it is time to cling to your images.
We delay and wail too much.

Do you hear or do you not the rattle of shields?   100

When, if not now, shall we hang
robes and garlands on your statues, supplicating?

I see the sound!
No one spear rattled so.

What will you do? Will you betray,
ancient lord of our land Ares,
your own land?

O spirit of the golden helmet look down upon us,
look down upon a city
which once you dearly loved.

City guarding gods of our land, come, come all of
   you!
Look upon us a band of virgins,   110
suppliants against slavery!
Around our city the wave of warriors, with waving
   plumes,
roars; blasts of the War God stirred them.
Alas alas Zeus, Father Omnipotent! all fulfilling!
Let us not fall into the hands of the foeman!

For the Argives are around Cadmus' city.   120
Fear is stronger than arms.
There is murder in the ringing bits
between their horses' jaws.
Seven proud captains of the host,
with harness and spear,
having won their place by lot,
stand champions at seven gates.
O victory, battle-loving, Zeus begotten,
save our city!

O Pallas, and the Horseman, Prince of the Sea, 130
King of the Trident, Poseidon,
deliverance from fear,
deliverance grant.
You, Ares, protect the city of Cadmus, that bears your
 name.

Show your care for it, in manifest presence.
And Cypris, who are our ancestress   140
turn destruction away. We are sprung from your
 blood
we approach you and cry
with prayers for the ears of the gods.

And you, Wolf God, be a very Wolf
in the enemy host. And you, daughter of Leto,
make ready your bow.

Ah, ah,   150
the rattle of chariots round the city: I hear it.
O Lady Hera,
the groaning axles of the loaded wheels.
Beloved Artemis!
The air is mad with the whirr of spears.
What will happen to our city, what will become of it,
whereto shall the gods bring an end upon us?

There comes a shower of stones on the top of the
 battlements!

O beloved Apollo!
There is the rattle of bronze-bound shields at our
    gates! 160
O Son of Zeus
from whom comes the war's fulfilment,
from whom comes the fight's holy consummation.

O Athene, Blessed Queen, Champion of the city,
deliver her from the assault of the Seven.
O gods all sufficient,
O gods and goddesses, Perfecters,
Protectors of our country's forts,
do not betray this city, spear-won,
to a foreign-tongued enemy. 170
Hear O hear the prayers, hand outstretched,
of the virgins supplicating in justice.

O beloved spirits,
that encompass our city to its deliverance,
show how much you love it:
Bethink you of the public sacrifices.
As we have thought of you, rescue us.
Remember, I pray you, the rites
with loving sacrifice offered. 180

Eteocles
You insupportable creatures, I ask you,
is this the best, is this for the city's safety,
is this enheartening for our beleaguered army,
to have you falling at the images
of the city's gods crying and howling,
an object of hatred for all temperate souls?
Neither in evils nor in fair good luck
may I share a dwelling with the tribe of women!
When she's triumphant, hers a confidence
past converse with another, when afraid
an evil greater both for home and city. 190
Here now running wild among the citizenry
you have roared them into spiritless cowardice.

So, outside of our gates, gains strength the enemy
while we are by ourselves, within, undone.
All this you may have, for living with women.
Now if there is anyone that will not hear
my orders, be he man or woman or in between,
sentence of death shall be decreed against him
and public stoning he shall not escape.
What is outside is a man's province: let no   200
woman debate it: within doors do no mischief!
Do you hear me or not? Or are you deaf?

Chorus
Dear son of Oedipus, the bumping rattle of the
      chariots,
rattle, rattle, I am afraid when I hear,
when the naves of the axles screech in their running
when the fire-forged bits speak ringingly,
rudder oars in horses' mouths.

Eteocles
What, shall the sailor, then, leave the stern
and run to the prow and find device for safety
when his vessel is foundering in the sea waves?   210

Chorus
But it was to the images of the gods
the ancient images I ran, trusting in the gods,
when the stony snowflakes crashed upon our gates:
nay, then I was lifted up with force and betook me
      to prayer
to the Blessed Ones, for our city,
that they may make their strength its protection.

Eteocles
For protection pray that our towers
hold off the enemy's spears.

Chorus
And shall not that be
as the gods dispose?

Eteocles
> The gods, they say,
of a captured town desert her.

Chorus
Never in my lifetime, never may this assembly
of gods desert us: never may I live to see   220
this city overrun, an enemy soldiery
putting the torch to it.

Eteocles
Do not call upon the gods
and then be guided wrongly.
Obedience is mother to success,
and success is parent of rescue—
so runs the proverb.

Chorus
This is true: but the strength of God is still greater.
Oftentimes when a man is hopelessly sunk
in misfortune He raises him, yes from his greatest
   sorrow
while the clouds still hang over him, high above our
   eyes.

Eteocles
But it is man's part, the sacrifice, the consultation   230
of the gods, when the enemy assault us;
it is yours to be silent and stay within doors.

Chorus
It is thanks to the gods that we have our city
unconquered: it is thanks to them
that our towers reject the mob of foemen.
What should be resented in these words?

Eteocles
I do not grudge your honoring the gods.
But lest you make our citizens cowards,
be quiet and not overfearful.

Chorus

It was but now that I heard the noise and the
  confusion
and trembling in fear came to this citadel,   240
sacred seat.

Eteocles

If you shall learn of men dying or wounded,
do not be eager to anticipate it with cries,
for murdered men are the War God's nourishment.

Chorus

The snorting of horses! There, I hear it.

Eteocles

Do not listen; do not hear too much.

Chorus

Our city groans from its foundation: we are surrounded.

Eteocles

I shall think of this: that is enough for you.

Chorus

I am afraid: the din at the gates grows louder.

Eteocles

Silence! Do not speak of this throughout the city.   250

Chorus

O Blessed Band, do not betray this fort.

Eteocles

Damnation! Can you not endure in silence?

Chorus

Fellow-citizen gods, grant me not to be a slave.

Eteocles

It is you who enslave yourselves, and all the city.

Chorus

O Zeus, All Mighty, your bolt upon our foes!

Eteocles
O Zeus, what a tribe you have given us in women!

Chorus
Base is the tribe of men of a captured town.

Eteocles
Words of ill omen, your hands on the images!

Chorus
Fear captures my tongue, and my spirit is nought.

Eteocles
Grant me, I pray you, the small thing I ask.   260

Chorus
Speak it quickly, that I may know.

Eteocles
Silence, you wretches, don't frighten your friends.

Chorus
I am silent: with others I'll endure what is fated.

Eteocles
I like this word better than those before.
Furthermore, get you away from the statues,
and being so, utter a better prayer:
"May the gods stand our allies." First hear my
prayer and then offer yours—
a holy gracious paean of thanksgiving,
the cry of sacrifice, our Grecian custom,
joy to our friends, dissolving fear of foes.   270

(*He approaches the images himself and prays.*)

Gods of the city, of this country gods,
Lords of its fields, and its assembly places,
Springs of Dirce, waters of Ismenus—
to you my vow:
if all go well with us, if the city is saved,
my people shall dye your hearths with the blood
of sacrificed sheep, aye with the blood

of bulls slaughtered to honor the gods.
I shall myself dedicate trophies,
spoils of my enemies, their garments fixed
on spear points, in your sanctuaries.

(*To the Chorus*)
These be your prayers, unlamenting   280
with no vain wild panting and moaning.
For all such you will not escape your doom.
I will take six men, myself to make a seventh
and go to post them at the city's gates,
opponents of the enemy, in gallant style,
before quick messengers are on us and
their words of haste burn us with urgency.

Chorus
I heed him but through fear
my spirit knows no sleep:
and neighbors to my heart,
anxieties, kindle terror   290
of the host that beleaguers us.
As the all-fearing dove
dreads for its nestlings' sake
the snakes that menace them.
For they against our forts
with all their host, with all their people,
come. What will become of me?
Jagged rocks they hurl
upon our citizens, on both sides pelted.   300
O children of Zeus, ye gods,
I pray you—protect
the city and the army,
the Cadmus born.
What country will you take in exchange,
than this one better,
if you abandon this deep-soiled land
to her enemies,
and Dirce's water, fairest to drink
of all that come from Poseidon   310

the Earth Upholder, and Tethys' sons?
Therefore, you city-guarding gods,
upon the men outside our forts
rain slaughtering destruction
and ruin, that will cast away their shields:
and for these citizens here
win glory and of the city   •
be the rescuers.
Then stand fair in your places   320
to receive our shrill prayers.

Pity it were that this city, so ancient,
should be cast to the House of Death,
a spear-booty, a slave,
in crumbling ashes, dishonorably,
sacked by an Achaean, with the gods' consent;
that its women be haled away,
captives, young and old,
dragged by the hair, as horses by the mane,
and their raiment torn about them.
Emptied the city wails   330
as the captive spoil, with mingled cries,
is led to its doom.
This heavy fate is what I fear.
It is a woeful thing for maidens unripe,
before the marriage rites, to tread
this bitter journey from their homes.
I would say that the dead
are better off than this.
Alas, unlucky indeed the fate
of a city captured—   340
murder, fire, and rapine,
all the city polluted by smoke,
and the breath of Ares on it
maddened, desecrating piety, slaying the people.

There is tumult through the town.
Against her comes a towering net.
Man stands against man with the spear and is killed.

Young mothers, blood-boltered,
cry bitterly for the babes at their breast.   350
The roving bands of pillagers are all brothers;
he that has plunder meets with another;
he that is empty calls him that is empty,
wishing to have a partner, eager for a share
neither less nor yet equal.
From such things what shall one augur?

All sorts of grain fallen
strewn on the ground vex,
embitter the eye of the housewife.
The great, profuse gifts of the earth   360
in reckless streams of waste are poured out.
The girls, new servants, new to misery,
must endure a war captive's bed,
bed of a man successful.
Theirs the expectation of night's consummation
but for a triumphant enemy
to help their tearful sorrow.

Half-Chorus
Here, I think, friends, your scout comes bringing
some news of the enemy—hastily urging   370
the joints of his legs to carry him here.

Half-Chorus
And here is the king himself, the son
of Oedipus in the nick of time to hear
the messenger's story. He too is in haste
and nimbly steps along.

Messenger
                    I can declare—
I know it well—the enemy's position:
how each at the gates has won by lot his station.
At the Proetid gate Tydeus now thunders
but dares not cross Ismenus' ford; the prophet
forbids. The sacrifices are unfavorable.
Tydeus, enraged and thirsting for the fight,   380

threatens, like serpents' hiss at noonday;
strikes with abuse the wise seer, Oecleides,
"battle and death make him cringe
through cowardice"—so he shouts aloud
and shakes his threefold shadowing plumes,
mane of his crested helm. Beneath his shield,
inside, ring brazen bells, a peal of terror,
and on the shield he bears this arrogant
device—a fashioned sky afire with stars.
In the shield's midst a glorious full moon,
night's eye, the eldest of the stars, stands out.   390
With such mad bragging and with overweening
trappings of war he roars along the banks
in love with battle, like the horse that chafes
against the bit, high mettled, impatient, hearing
the trumpet's sound. Against this champion
whom will you set?
When the bolts are shot back at the Proetid gates,
who will be champion fit to deserve our trust?

Eteocles
No equipment of a man will make me tremble.
Devices on a shield deal no one wounds.
The plumes and bells bite not without the spear.
And for this night you speak of on his shield   400
glistening with all the stars of heaven—someone
may find his folly prophetic to himself.
For if in death night fall upon his eyes,
to him that bears this pompous blazonry
it shall be truly and most justly pregnant,
and he shall make his insolence prophesy
against himself.
         I nominate against him
as champion of these gates to challenge Tydeus,
the worthy son of Astacus—right noble,
one honoring the throne of Modesty
and hating insolent words.   410
Laggard in all things base he is wont to be

but not a coward. From those sown men
whom Ares spared his root springs—very native
is Melanippus to this land. His deeds
shall Ares with his dice determine;
but Justice, blood of his blood, sends him forth,
surely, to turn the enemy's spear away
from the mother that has borne him.

Chorus
May the gods grant
good luck to our champion,
since justly he comes forward
a fighter for us.
But I fear for our friends   420
to look upon bloodshed
of those we love, dying.

Messenger
Yes, may the gods grant him good luck.
At Electra's gates stands by lot Capaneus,
a giant this man, taller than the other,
and his threats breathe inhuman arrogance.
Our towers he menaces with terrors—Fortune
fulfil them not!—for he declares he'll sack
our city with the gods' good will or ill.
Not even Zeus's wrath striking the earth
before him shall be obstacle to his purpose.
The lightnings and the thunderbolts he likened   430
to the sun's warm rays at noontide.
His device a naked man that carries fire,
in his hands, ablaze, a torch all ready. In gold
are letters that declare "I'll burn the city."
Against this man send—who will meet him?
Who will abide his threats and never tremble?

Eteocles
This man's boasts, too, beget us other gain.
For of the haughtiness of vain men, true
accuser proves their own tongue. Capaneus

threatens to do—and is prepared to do—   440
disdains the gods, and giving exercise
to his mouth, in vain joy, up to heaven
mortal though he is, against Zeus sends his words,
shouted in swelling pride. I trust on him
will justly come the bolt that carries fire
in no way like the sun's warm rays at noontide.
Against him, be his lips never so insolent,
a man of fiery spirit shall be stationed,
strong Polyphontes, a guard trustworthy,
by favor of protecting Artemis
and of the other gods. Tell me another   450
that has his place by lot at another gate.

Chorus
Destruction on him that against the city
vaunts huge threats;
may the thunderbolt's blast restrain him
before he burst into my house,
before he ravish me from my maiden room.

Messenger
Now I shall tell him that by lot won next
station at the gates. The third lot cast
jumped from the upturned brazen helmet
in favor of a third man, Eteoclus,
that he should lead his regiment in a charge   460
against the gates of Neïs. He wheels his mares
snorting in their nose bands, ready to charge the gate.
Pipes on the bridle bands filled with insolent
nostril breath whistle in a foreign note.
His shield, too, has its design—and that no lowly—
a man in armor mounts a ladder's steps
to the enemy's town to sack it. Loud
cries also this man in his written legend
"Ares himself shall not cast me from the tower."
Against him send some champion trustworthy   470
to turn the yoke of slavery from this city.

Eteocles
This man I'll send and may good luck go with him!

There, he is gone. His boast is in his hands
Megareus, Creon's son, and of the seed
and race of the sown men. He will not blench
at the furious neighing of horses nor yield the gates.
Either by death he'll pay his nurture's due
to his own land or he will capture two men
and city as depicted on the shield
and crown his father's house with the spoils of war.
On with another's boasts—don't grudge me the story.   480

Chorus
Good success to you, I pray,
Champion of my house,
and to the enemy ill success!
as with wild extravagance
they prate against the city
with maddened heart, so may Zeus
the Avenger look on them in wrath.

Messenger
Another, the fourth, holds the gate that neighbors
Onca Athena, and takes his station with a shout,
Hippomedon's vast frame and giant form.
He whirled a disc around—I mean the circle
of his shield—until I shuddered. I speak truth.   490
The armorer cannot have been a poor one
that put upon the shield this work of art—
a Typho hurling from his fiery mouth
black smoke, the flickering sister of fire.
The rim that ran around the hollow boss
of the shield is solid wrought with coiling snakes.
The man himself cried out his warcry, he,
inspired by Ares, revels in violence
like a Bacchanal with murder in his glance.
Take good heed how you deal with such a man;
he boasts even now at the gate he will raise panic.   500

Eteocles

First Onca Pallas, with her place beside
our city, neighbor to our gates, will hate
the fellow's violence and keep him off,
as it were a chill snake from her nestling brood.
And then Hyperbius, the stout son of Oenops,
has been chosen to match him man for man, right
    willing,
at fortune's need, to put his fate to question—
no man to be reproached either in form
or spirit or in bearing of his arms.
Hermes has matched the two with excellent reason,
for man with man they shall engage as foes
and on their shields shall carry enemy gods.   510
The one has Typho breathing fire, the other,
Hyperbius, has father Zeus in station
sitting upon his shield, and in his hand
a burning bolt.
No one has yet seen Zeus defeated anywhere.
Such on each side are the favors of the gods;
we are on the winning side, they with the vanquished
if Zeus than Typho mightier prove in battle.   520

Chorus

Sure am I that he who hath
Zeus's foe upon his shield
the unloved form of the earth-born God,
the likeness hated by men
and the long-living gods,
shall lay his head before our gates.

Messenger

So may it prove. Now I shall take the fifth
that has his station at the fifth, the Northern gate,
right by Amphion's tomb that sprung from Zeus.
By his lance he swears—and with sure confidence
he holds it more in reverence than a god,   530
more precious than his eyes—he will sack the town
of Thebes in despite of Zeus. Such the loud vaunt

of this creature sprung of a mountain mother,
    handsome,
something between man and boy.
The beard is newly sprouting on his cheeks,
the thick, upspringing hair of youth in its bloom.
His spirit unlike his maiden name* is savage,
and with a grim regard he now advances.
He too boasts high as he draws near our gates.
For on his brazen shield, his body's rounded
defense, he swings an insult to our city,   540
the Sphinx that ate men raw, cunningly wrought,
burnished, embossed, secured with rivets there.
A man she bears beneath her, a Cadmaean,
so that at him most of our darts shall fly.
When he comes to the battle, so it seems,
he will not play the petty shopkeeper
nor shame the course of his long journey here—
Parthenopeaus of Arcadia.
He lives among our enemy presently
and pays to Argos a fair wage for his keep,
with threats against our forts—which God fulfil not.

Eteocles

Would that they might obtain what from the gods   550
they pray against us—them, and their impious boasts.
Then would they perish utterly and ill.
We have a man to encounter your Arcadian,
a man unboasting but his hand looks for
the thing that should be done—Actor, the brother
of him I spoke of earlier. He will not suffer
a heedless tongue to flow within our gates
and to breed mischief, nor to cross our walls,
one bearing on an enemy shield the likeness
of the most hateful Sphinx—or else the beast
borne outside shall have cause of blame against   560
him that would carry her in, for many a hammering

---

* Parthenopeaus: Maiden One.

blow she will get beneath the city's walls.
With the God's will, I may indeed speak truth.

Chorus
The words go through my heart;
the hair stands upright on my head;
as I listen to mighty words
of impious boasting men.
May the gods destroy them within our land!

Messenger
A sixth I'll tell you of—a most modest man
greatest in might of battle, yet a prophet,
strong Amphiaraus, at the Homoloian gates   570
stationed, shouts insults at strong Tydeus: "Murderer,
cause of confusion to the city, greatest
teacher of evil to Argos; of the Fury
a summoning herald; servant of bloodshed;
adviser to Adrastus of all these evils."
And then again with eyes uplifted calling
on your own brother, strong prince Polyneices,
he dwells twice on the latter part of his name.*
And this is the speech to which his lips give utter-
    ance:
"Is such a deed as this dear to the gods,   580
and fair to hear and tell of, for posterity,
for one to sack his native city, destroy
the gods of his country, bringing in
an alien enemy host?
                    What justice
shall quench the spring of guilt of another murder?
Your fatherland destroyed by the spear
which your own zeal impelled—shall it be your ally?
But for myself I shall make fat this soil
a prophet buried under enemy ground.
Let us fight. The fate I look for is right honorable."
So spoke the prophet brandishing his round   590

* The latter half of the Greek word Polyneices means "strife."

brazen shield. No device is on its circle.
He is best not at seeming to be such
but being so. Deep indeed is the furrow
of his mind from which he gathers fruit, and good
the counsels that do spring from it. For him
send out, I recommend, wise and good challengers,
for he is dangerous who reveres the gods.

Eteocles
Alas, the luck which among human beings
conjoins an honest man with impious wretches!
In every enterprise is no greater evil
than bad companionship: there is no fruit   600
that can be gathered. The field of doom
bears death as its harvest.
Indeed, a pious man, going on board
as shipmate of a crew of rascal sailors
and of some mischief they have perpetrated,
has often died with the God-detested breed;
or a just man, with fellow citizens
themselves inhospitable, forgetful of the gods,
has fallen into the same snare as the unrighteous,
and smitten by the common scourge of God
has yielded up his life.
                              Even so this seer,
this son of Oecles, wise, just, good, and holy,   610
a prophet mighty, mingling with the impious—
against his better reason—with loud-mouthed
men who pursue a road long to retrace,
with God's will shall be dragged to their general doom.
I think he will not even assault the gate—
not that he is a coward or faint of spirit—
but well he knows how he must die in the battle
if Loxias' prophecies shall bear fruit.
Loxias either says nothing or speaks seasonably.
Yet against him, the strong prince Lasthenes   620
we shall range in combat, an inhospitable

sentry, in mind an old man but a young one
in his body's vigor, in his swift-swooping charge,
in his hand, undelaying to snatch a spear
and hurl it against the unprotected shield side.
But success—that is for men the gift of God alone.

Chorus
Hear, O ye gods, our lawful prayers
and bring them to fulfilment that
the city prosper, averting
the horrors of war upon our invaders.
May Zeus strike them and slay them
with his bolt outside of our walls.   630

Messenger
Lo, now, the seventh at the seventh gate
I shall unfold—your own, your very brother.
Hear how he curses the city and what fate
he invokes upon her. He prays that once his feet
are set upon her walls, once he is proclaimed
a conqueror of this land, once he has cried
paean of triumph in its overthrow,
he then may close in fight with you and killing
may find his death beside your corpse.
Or if you live, that he may banish you—
in the selfsame way as you dishonored him—
to exile. So he shouts and calls the gods
of his race and of his fatherland to witness   640
his prayers—a very violent Polyneices.
He bears a new-made, rounded shield
and a twofold device contrived thereon:
a woman leading modestly a man
conducts him, pictured as a warrior,
wrought all in gold. She claims she is Justice,
and the inscription reads: I will bring him home
and he shall have his city and shall walk
in his ancestral house.
                              Such are the signs.
But you yourself determine whom to send.   650

You shall not find a fault in my report:
but you determine how to steer the state.

Eteocles
Our race, our race, the race of Oedipus,
by the gods maddened, by them greatly hated;
alas, my father's curses are now fulfilled!
But for me no crying and no lamentation
lest even sorer sorrow be begotten.
I tell you, Polyneices, so well named,
soon we shall know the pertinence of your sign,
whether your golden characters on the shield,   660
babbling, in wild distraction of the mind,
will indeed bring you home. This might have been,
if Justice, Zeus's virgin daughter had stood
by his actions and his mind. But in his flight
out of the darkness of his mother's womb,
in his growth as a child, in his young manhood,
in the first gathering of his chin's hair—no, never
did Justice look upon him nor regard him.
I do not think that now he comes to outrage
this fatherland of his she will stand his ally,
or else she is called falsely Justice, joining   670
with a man whose mind conceives no limit in villainy.
In this I trust and to the conflict with him
I'll go myself. What other has more right?
King against king, and brother against brother,
foe against foe we'll fight.
                              Bring me my greaves
to shield me from the lances and the stones.

Chorus
O dearest son of Oedipus, do not
be like in temper to this utterer
of dreadful sayings. There are enough Cadmaeans
to grapple with the Argives: such blood is expiable.   680
But for the blood of brothers mutually shed
there is no growing old of the pollution.

Eteocles
If a man suffer ill, let it be without shame;
this is the only gain when we are dead.
For deeds both evil and disgraceful never
will you say word of good.

Chorus
What do you long for, child?
Let not the frantic lust
for battle, filling the heart
carry you away. Expel
the evil passion at its birth.

Eteocles
It is the God that drives this matter on.
Since it is so—on, on with favoring wind   690
this wave of hell that has engulfed for its share
all kin of Laius, whom Phoebus has so hated.

Chorus
Bitter-biting indeed
is the passion that urges you
to accomplish manslaying,
bitter in fruit,
where the blood to be shed is unlawful.

Eteocles
Yes, for the hateful black
curse of my father loved
sits on my dry and tearless eyes
and tells me first of gain and then of death.

Chorus
Resist its urging: coward
you shall not be called
if you rule your life well.
Forth from your house the black-robed Fury   700
shall go, when from your hands
the gods shall receive a sacrifice.

Eteocles
We are already past the care of gods.
For them our death is the admirable offering.
Why then delay, fawning upon our doom?

Chorus
Not when the chance is yours—
for in the veering change
of spirit though late
perhaps the God may change
and come with kinder breath.
Now his blast is full.

Eteocles
The curse of Oedipus has fanned that blast.
Too true the vision of sleepy nightmares   710
showing division of my father's heritage.

Chorus
Listen to women though you like it not.

Eteocles
Speak then of what may be. Nor should it be long.

Chorus
Go not you, go not, to the seventh gate.

Eteocles
No words of yours will blunt my whetted purpose.

Chorus
Yet even bad victory the gods hold in honor.

Eteocles
No soldier may endure to hear such words.

Chorus
Do you wish to reap as harvest a brother's blood?

Eteocles
If gods give ill, no man may shun their giving.

Chorus

I shudder at the Goddess,   720
unlike all other gods,
who compasses destruction of the house,
utterly unforgetting, prophet of ill,
the Fury invoked by a father's curse.
I dread that it bring to pass
the furious invocations
of Oedipus astray in his mind.
This strife, death to his sons, spurs it on.

A stranger grants them land-allotment,
a Chalyb, Scythian colonist,
a bitter divider of possessions—
iron-hearted Steel.   730
Yes, he has allotted them land to dwell in
as much as the dead may possess:
no share theirs of their broad acres.

When they die with mutual hand
mutually slaughtering
and earth's dust shall drink
black clotted murder-blood,
who shall then give purification,
who shall wash away the stain?
O new evils of the house,   740
new mingled with the old.

Old is the tale of sin I tell
but swift in retribution:
to the third generation it abides.
Thrice in Pythian prophecies
given at Navel-of-Earth
Apollo had directed
King Laius all issueless to die
and save his city so . . .

but he was mastered by loving folly   750
and begot for himself a doom,
father-murdering Oedipus,

who sowed his mother's sacred womb,
whence he had sprung himself,
with bloody root, to his heartbreak.
Madness was the coupler
of this distracted pair.

Now, as it were, a sea
drives on the wave:
one sinks, another rises,   760
triple-crested around the prow
of the city, and breaks in foam.
Our defense between is but a little thing
no bigger than a wall in width.
I fear that with our princes
our city be subdued.

For heavy is the settlement
of ancient curses, to fulfilment brought.
That evil when fulfilled
passes not away.
Prosperity grown over fat
of men, gain seeking,   770
compels jettisoning
of all goods, utterly.

What man has earned such admiration
of gods and men that shared his city
and of the general throng of mortal men,
as Oedipus—who ever had such honor
as he that from his land had banished
the Sphinx, that ate men up?

But when in misery he knew
the meaning of his dreadful marriage,
in pain distraught, in heart distracted   780
he brought a double sorrow to fulfilment.
With patricidal hand
he reft himself of eyes
that dearer to him were than his own children.
And on those children savage

117

maledictions he launched
for their cruel tendance of him
and wished they might divide
with iron-wielding hand his own possessions.
And now I fear   790
that nimble-footed Fury bring those wishes to fulfil-
    ment.

Messenger
Take heart, you mother's darlings, this your city
has escaped the yoke of slavery. Fallen
are the vauntings of the monstrous men.
Our city is in smooth water and though many
the assaults of the waves, has shipped no sea.
Our wall still stands protecting us, our gates
we barricaded with trustworthy champions.
For the most part all is well—at six of the gates.
The seventh the Lord Apollo, Captain of Sevens,*   800
took to himself: on Oedipus' race
he has fulfilled Laius' ancient follies.

Chorus
What new and evil thing concerns the city?

Messenger
The city is saved, but the twin princes—

Chorus
Who? What do you mean? Through fear of your
    words I am frantic.

Messenger
Get your wits and hear. Oedipus' two sons—

Chorus
Alas, alas, the ills I prophesied.

Messenger
In very truth, crushed to the ground.   810

---

* "Captain of Sevens" is an ancient cult title of Apollo.

Chorus
They lie there? Bitter though it be, yet speak.

Messenger
The men have fallen, one another's killers.

Chorus
Did brothers' hands achieve a mutual murder?

Messenger
The ground has drunk the blood shed each by each.

Chorus
So all too equal was their guiding spirit.

Messenger
Surely he destroys this most unlucky race.
Here is store of sorrow and joy at once.
The city has good fortune, but its lords,
the two generals, have divided the possessions
with hammered steel of Scythia. They shall have
what land suffices for a grave, swept thither
down the wind of their father's ill-boding curses.   820

Chorus
O great Zeus and Spirits that guard
the city, you Protectors
that guard our walls:
shall I rejoice, shall I cry aloud
for our city's safety?
or for those wretched ones, luckless and childless,
our generals, shall I lament?
They have earned their name too well
and "men of strife" they have perished   830
through impious intent.

O black curse consummated
on the race, the curse of Oedipus!
An evil chill assails my heart.
I raise the dirge at the tomb
like a Bacchanal, hearing

of their blood-dripping corpses,
of their ill-fated death.
Ill-omened indeed
is this melody of the Spear.

It has worked to an end, not failed,   840
the curses called on them by their father of old.
The decisions of Laius, wanting in faith,
have had effect till now.
My heart is troubled for the city;
divine warnings are not blunted.
O full of sorrows, this you have done
a deed beyond belief.
Woes worthy of groaning
have come in very truth.

(*The bodies of the princes are carried in, escorted
       by their two sisters, Ismene and Antigone.*)

Here is visible evidence of the messenger's tale.
Twofold our griefs and double
the ills these two men wrought;
double the fated sorrow
now brought to fulfilment.   850
What shall I say but that
here sorrows, sorrows' children,
abide at the hearth of the house?
But, my friends, down the wind of groans
with hands that beat the head
ply the speeding stroke
which sends through Death's waters
the dark-sailed ship of mission
to the shore, untrodden by Apollo, and sunless,
the shore unseen, that welcomes all at last.   860
Here they come to their bitter task,
Ismene and Antigone,
to make the dirge for their brothers.
With true sincerity, I think,
from their deep bosoms,

they shall utter a song of grief that fits the cause.
Us it concerns to sing,
before their song,
the ill-sounding Furies' dirge,
and the hateful Hades paean.   870

O most luckless of all women
that fasten the girdle about their robes,
I cry, I groan: there is no guile
in my heart to check my true dirge.

Antigone (*speaking over the bodies*)
O you misguided ones,
faithless to friends, unwearied in evil,
you who plundered your father's house
to your misery, with the spear.

Chorus
Wretched indeed those who wretched death
have found to the ruin of their house.   880

Ismene
O you that tore the roof
from our house, you that glimpsed
the bitter sovereignty, at last
you are reconciled—by the sword.

Chorus
Too truly has that dread spirit,
the Fury of Oedipus,
brought all this to fulfilment.

Antigone
Stricken through the left sides
stricken indeed,
through sides born of a common mother.   890
Alas, strange ones,
alas for the curse
of death that answered death!

Chorus
A straight thrust to house and body
delivered by unspeakable wrath,
by the doom invoked by a father's curse,
which they shared without discord.

Ismene
Through the city the cry of weeping;
the walls groan aloud;   900
the plain that loved them groans aloud.
There abide for their descendants
the possessions for which
their bitter fate was paid,
for which their strife arose,
for which they found the end of death.

Chorus
In bitterness of heart they shared
their possessions in equality:
no blame from friends
has their arbitrator,
Ares, impartial to both sides.   910

Antigone
By the stroke of the sword they are as they are.
By the stroke of the sword there awaits them—what?
The share in their ancestral tomb, says someone.

Chorus
A shrill cry escorts them from their house,
a cry heartrending,
a cry for its own griefs, its own woes,
in anguish of mind with no thought of joy,   920
weeping tears from a heart that breaks,
for these our two princes.

Ismene
One may say over the bodies
of this unhappy pair:
much they have done to their fellow citizens,

and much to all the ranks of foreigners
who died in this destructive war.

Chorus
Unlucky she that bore them
above all womankind
that are called by a mother's name.
She took as husband her own child
and bore these who have died   930
their brotherly hands working each other's murder.

Antigone
Brotherly indeed in utter destruction
in unkindly severance,
in frantic strife,
in the ending of their quarrel.

Chorus
Their enmity is ended, in the earth
blood-drenched their life is mingled.
Very brothers are they now.   940
Bitter the reconciler of their feud,
stranger from over the sea,
sped hither by the fire,
whetted steel.
A bitter and evil divider of possessions,
Ares, who made their father's curse
a thing of utter truth.

Ismene
They have their share, unhappy ones
of Zeus given sorrows:
beneath their bodies, earth
in fathomless wealth shall lie.   950

Chorus (*speaking over the bodies*)
You who have made your race
blossom with many woes:
over you at last have cried
the Curses their shrill lament,

and the race is turned to confusion and rout.
The trophy of Destruction stands
at the gates where they were smitten
and conqueror of the two
the Spirit at last has come to rest.   960

(The dirge proper. The sisters stand each at the head
of one of the corpses.)

Antigone
You smote and were smitten.

Ismene
You killed and were slain.

Antigone
By the spear you killed.

Ismene
By the spear you died.

Antigone
Wretched in acting.

Ismene
Wretched in suffering.

Antigone
Let the groans go forth.

Ismene
Let the tears fall.

Antigone
You lie in death—

Ismene
having killed—

Antigone and Ismene
Woe, woe.

Antigone
My mind is distraught with groans.

Ismene
With groans my heart is full.

Antigone
Alas, alas, creature of tears.

Ismene
Alas, again, all-miserable.   970

Antigone
By a loving hand you died.

Ismene
And killed one that loved you.

Antigone
A double sorrow to relate.

Ismene
A double sorrow to see.

Antigone
Two sorrows hard by one another.

Ismene
Brother's sorrow close to brother's.

Chorus
O wretched Fate, giver of heaviness,
awful shade of Oedipus,
black Fury,
verily a spirit mighty in strength!

Ismene and Antigone
Woe, woe.

Antigone
Evils unfit to look upon—

Ismene
have you shown after banishment.

Antigone
He came not back when he had slain.   980

Ismene
This one saved, lost his own life.

Antigone
This one died—

Ismene
and killed the other.

Antigone
Race unhappy.

Ismene
Deed unhappy.

Antigone
Grievous sorrows of kindred.

Ismene
Grievous, thrice grievous sorrow.

Chorus
O wretched Fate, giver of heaviness,
awful shade of Oedipus,
black Fury,
verily a spirit mighty in strength.

Antigone
You have learned the lesson by experience.

Ismene
And you have learned it, no whit later.   990

Antigone
When you returned to the city—

Ismene
yes, to face him with your spear.

Antigone
Deadly to tell.

Ismene
Deadly to see.

Antigone
Pain—

Ismene
Ill—

Antigone
To house and land—

Ismene
and most of all to me.

Antigone
O unhappy king of sorrow!

Ismene
O of all most rich in pain!   1000

Antigone
Where shall we lay them in the earth?

Ismene
Where their honor is greatest.

Antigone
O brothers possessed by evil spirits, in doom—

Ismene
that will sleep by the side of their father to his hurt.

Herald
It is my duty to declare to you,
counselors of the people, the resolves
already taken and the present pleasure
of this Cadmaean city. . . .
Our Lord Eteocles for his loyalty
it is determined to bury in the earth
that he so loved. Fighting its enemies
he found his death here. In the sight
of his ancestral shrines he is pure and blameless   1010
and died where young men die right honorably.
These are my instructions to communicate

with respect to him. His brother Polyneices,
or rather his dead body, you must cast out
unburied, for the dogs to drag and tear
as fits one who would have destroyed our country
had not some God proved obstacle to his spear.
Even in death he shall retain this guilt
against his gods ancestral whom he dishonored
when he brought his foreign host here for invasion
and would have sacked the city. So it is resolved
that he shall have, as his penalty, a burial   1020
granted dishonorably by the birds of the air
and that no raising of a mound by hand
attend him nor observance of keening dirge.
Unhonored shall his funeral be by friends.
This is the pleasure of the Cadmaean state.

Antigone
So I to the Cadmaean magistrates
declare: if no one else will dare to join me
in burying him, yet will I bury him
and take the danger on my head alone
when that is done. He is my brother. I
am not ashamed of this anarchic act   1030
of disobedience to the city. Strange,
a strange thing is the common blood we spring from—
a mother wretched, a father doomed to evil.
Willingly then with one that would not will it,
live spirit with dead man in sisterhood
I shall bear my share. His flesh
the hollow-bellied wolves shall never taste of.
Let that be no one's "pleasure or decree."
His tomb and burying place I will contrive
though but a woman. In the bosom folds
of my linen robe I shall carry earth to him.
And I shall cover him: let no one determine
the contrary. Be of good cheer (*to her sister*), I shall   1040
find means to bring my will to pass.

Herald
                              I forbid
this act, defiance of the city's pleasure.

Antigone
I forbid you your superfluous proclamations.

Herald
Harsh is the people now that danger's past.

Antigone
Harsh truly. But *he* shall not go unburied.

Herald
Him the state hates, will you grace with a tomb?

Antigone
Long since the gods determined of his honor.

Herald
Not till he cast in peril this land of ours.

Antigone
He suffered ill and gave back what he suffered.

Herald
This deed of his was aimed at all, not one.   1050

Antigone
Last of the gods Contention ends her tale.
But I shall bury him: spare me long speech.

Herald
Have your own way: but I forbid the act.

Chorus
Alas, alas.
O high-vaunting, ruin to the race
fatal Furies, who have destroyed
the race of Oedipus so utterly—
What will happen to me? What shall I do?
What shall I plan?
How shall I be so heartless,

not to mourn for you,
not to give escort to your funeral?
But I fear the dreadful authority   1060
of the people: I am turned from my purpose.

(*To the body of Eteocles*)
Many mourners you shall win:

(*To the body of Polyneices*)
But this poor wretch unwept
save for his sister's single dirge
shall go his road. Who would yield
so much obedience as this?

                              (*The Chorus divides in two.*)

First Half-Chorus
Let the state do or not
what it will to the mourners of Polyneices.
We will go and bury him;
we will go as his escort.
This grief is common to the race   1070
but now one way and now another
the city approves the path of justice.

Second Half-Chorus
But we will go with the other, as the city
and Justice jointly approve.
For after the Blessed Ones and the strength of Zeus
he is the one who saved the city
from utter destruction, from being overwhelmed
by the wave of foreign invaders.

PROMETHEUS BOUND

Translated by David Grene

INTRODUCTION TO
PROMETHEUS BOUND

IN THE eighteenth century the critics knew what they thought about the *Prometheus* of Aeschylus and knew why they thought it. It was a bad play because the structure was episodic, the characters extravagant and improbable, the diction uncouth and wild. Their handbook of criticism was the *Poetics* of Aristotle, either directly or indirectly drawn upon. And it is plain that the Aeschylean play does not measure up to Aristotelian standards. Since the eighteenth-century critics believed there was only one canon for drama, rooted in the principles of Aristotle, they quite reasonably judged the *Prometheus* a bad play. During the nineteenth century, with the Romantic revival and the breakdown of the so-called "classical" rules of the drama, the *Prometheus* was acclaimed by the critics as a great work of art. But they so acclaimed it entirely in terms of its theme or its poetry and in the same breath spoke of the greatness of Sophocles' *Oedipus*, Shakespeare's *Hamlet*, and Goethe's *Faust*. There was no effort to discover what in the nature of Aeschylus' dramatic method set him so apart from Sophocles that the eighteenth-century critics had refused to recognize his merit. Nor did they sift the striking differences which exist between the *Prometheus* and any of the Shakespearean tragedies or *Faust*. They contented themselves with vague and not entirely satisfied references to the *Prometheus* as a study-drama rather than a play for the theater.

Of the three dramatists, Aeschylus perhaps appears for a modern reader the most provocative and the most enigmatic. There is so much in the *Oresteia*, for instance, and particularly in the *Agamemnon*, which appeals directly to our sense

of the theater and dramatic poetry. And yet the conclusion
with its stress on an obscure theological point and its very
local emphasis on the court of the Areopagus baffles our
awakened interest. But in no play of Aeschylus is a reader
today so aware at the same time of the directness and uni-
versality of the theme and also of the purely Greek, and indeed purely fifth-century, implications of it as in the *Prometheus*. The remarks that follow constitute only one more
attempt among many to assist readers who are not classical
scholars to a more complete understanding of a very great
and very puzzling play.

For Aeschylus the myth is the illustration of a great per-
manent truth that he finds at the heart of man's activity.
His dramatic imagination seizes on such truths as are most
frequently a compromise between two opposites, and consequently the myths he uses most are those which tell of conflict on a cosmic scale and conflict ultimately laid by some
concessions on the part of both combatants. To make myth
universally significant, both characters and plot must correspond symbolically with characters and plot on one or
more levels in addition to the myth in which they are im-
bedded.

In the *Prometheus*, the probability is not in the action or
the conditions the dramatist has stated for us before the
play commences. It consists in setting forth a very simple
story, one which comes from a common stock of mytholog-
ical stories known to almost all, and fusing this with a number of other patterns known to almost all. Everybody in
Greece knew the legend of the Titan who stole fire from
heaven to give it to man. But everybody in Greece also knew
the story of Peisistratus, the tyrant of Athens, or Lygdamis,
the tyrant of Naxos, or Polycrates, the tyrant of Samos. They
knew the kind of outrage citizens had suffered at their
hands, the innovations in established custom and ritual and
in the conventional governmental attitudes of mercy, the
"unwritten laws." Thus when the Prometheus-Zeus conflict
is represented also as the rebel versus tyrant conflict, it has

been invested with a new probability. And men everywhere have felt, some obscurely and some clearly, an opposition between the animal and the spirit in man, between violence and persuasion, between might and intellect. So when the Zeus-Lygdamis versus Prometheus-rebel struggle is represented as another facet of the conflict between the two most powerful factors in human life—brute force and mind—the story has been invested with a new probability drawn from the community of man's experience. And men everywhere have known the torture of subjugation to a stronger force than themselves, have known the helplessness of persuasion against force, and yet have believed in the ultimate triumph of persuasion. And so, when the suffering Prometheus cries out in his helplessness and his knowledge, and doubts yet feels certain of the outcome, the story has been invested with a new probability drawn from the community of man's experience. The original story of Zeus and Prometheus is like a stone thrown into a quiet pool, where the ripples spread in wider and wider circles.

Methods like the Aeschylean, developed to varying degrees of complexity, are familiar in other forms of literature. The degree of complexity is determined by the number of levels of meaning involved. For instance, in the *Pilgrim's Progress*, there is only one meaning in the tale apart from the highly dramatic story of Christian's journey, and that is the progress of the Christian soul toward the Eternal City. But, in the *Prometheus*, Aeschylus has made his story significant on a number of different levels, though each level involves the conflict of two opposing principles. For Prometheus is, politically, the symbol of the rebel against the tyrant who has overthrown the traditional rule of Justice and Law. He is the symbol of Knowledge against Force. He is symbolically the champion of man, raising him through the gift of intelligence, against the would-be destroyer of man. Finally, there is a level at which Prometheus is symbolically Man as opposed to God.

We are never told in this play why Zeus wished to destroy

man. There is no indication what sort of animal he wished
to put in his place; but, insofar as Prometheus in disobedience to Zeus enlightened man by the gift of intelligence, it
may be assumed that Zeus's creation would have had no
such dangerous potentialities of development. This first attempt to destroy mankind is almost certainly the flood of
Deucalion, of which we hear elsewhere, and there is a tradition to the effect that Prometheus counseled Deucalion to
the building of the ark which preserved him and his family.
The second action in Prometheus' rescue of man from the
enmity of the world in which he found himself is even more
significant. "I stopped mortals from foreseeing doom," says
Prometheus.

> *Chorus*: What cure did you provide them with against
> that sickness?
>
> *Prometheus*: I placed in them blind hopes.
>
> *Chorus*: That was a great gift you gave to men.

As the rest of his gifts to man are all concerned with
enlightenment, and, indeed, as fire itself becomes a symbol
of that enlightenment, this gift of "blind hopes" seems at
first strange. Yet it is quite consistent. There is a passage in
the *Gorgias* which is illuminating here. We are told that in
the days of Kronos and *when Zeus was newly king*, men
were informed as to the day of their death and were judged
alive, with all their clothes on and their possessions about
them, by live judges. This was a practice which brought
much injustice, says Plato, and Zeus ultimately ordered it
otherwise. Plato is using the myth for the illustration of his
own theme, and we must not be surprised that his picture of
the development of man when this was the state of things
does not accord with that of Aeschylus. But the dating in
the case of Plato shows either that he and Aeschylus were
drawing on the same myth or else that Plato is borrowing
from Aeschylus: "In the days of Kronos and when Zeus was
newly king." What, then, is the meaning of the blind hopes

which were the compensation for man's loss of knowledge of his death and yet left him able to use his reason to build houses and yoke horses and invent cures for sickness?

Prometheus is wise in the wisdom of his mother Themis, or Earth, and consequently wise in the knowledge of destiny. This is not reason. It is absolute knowledge. The knowledge of the day of a man's death partakes of that quality, for it is in the province of destiny. Thus man at the beginning had an infinitely small particle of the *same kind of knowledge* which Prometheus enjoyed in large measure. Just as animals today seem to have a curious intuition of the coming of their death and crawl away into hiding to face it, so primitive man had this knowledge. And Prometheus caused them to cease to foreknow the day of their death. For the gift of reason, the supreme ally in their struggle against nature, made them fight on against death in "blind hope," even when the day of their death had come. It is worth noticing here that, of the two accounts of man's origins in the world—the one that of a golden age of material and moral perfection and the other of miserable ignorance and helplessness—Aeschylus has preferred the scientific tradition. But he has chosen to incorporate in his account a grain of the truth of the former. The very small particle of divine. The fire itself, Prometheus' greatest and most celebrated gift to man, is a symbol of practical, not speculative, reason. And nowhere does Aeschylus assert that such speculative reason in its full will ever be in man's possession.

There is a sense in which Prometheus in this play appeals directly to the human sympathies of his audience because though a Titan and a God his helplessness before Zeus places him on the same level with mortals. It is the story of the man-god who must suffer for his kindness to man by having his state equated with theirs. In the case of Prometheus the good achieved for man is achieved before the suffering—which comes in the nature of a punishment. The cry of Prometheus—

I knew when I transgressed nor will deny it.
In helping man I brought my troubles on me;
but yet I did not think that with such tortures
I should be wasted on these airy cliffs—

is the cry of one who is man enough to be weak under pain. Prometheus, though possessed of a knowledge of destiny and therefore of victory in the end, is for the present at the mercy of a brutal and ignorant opponent. So, too, is the mortal Io. So are all the mortals over whom Death holds power against which they fight with "blind hopes." Finally, Prometheus' deliverance by Heracles, who is part god and part man, once again binds his fate to the creature whom he has helped to survive in the teeth of the opposition of the supreme god.

CHARACTERS

Might

Violence (*muta persona*)

Hephaestus

Prometheus

Oceanos

Io

Hermes

Chorus of daughters of Oceanos

PROMETHEUS BOUND

SCENE: *A bare and desolate crag in the Caucasus.*
Enter Might and Violence, demons, servants
of Zeus, and Hephaestus, the smith.

Might

This is the world's limit that we have come to; this
is the Scythian country, an untrodden desolation.
Hephaestus, it is you that must heed the commands
the Father laid upon you to nail this malefactor to the
high craggy rocks in fetters unbreakable of adamantine chain. For it was your flower, the brightness of
fire that devises all, that he stole and gave to mortal
men; this is the sin for which he must pay the gods
the penalty—that he may learn to endure and like   10
the sovereignty of Zeus and quit his man-loving disposition.

Hephaestus

Might and Violence, in you the command of Zeus has
its perfect fulfilment: in you there is nothing to
stand in its way. But, for myself, I have not the
heart to bind violently a God who is my kin here on
this wintry cliff. Yet there is constraint upon me to
have the heart for just that, for it is a dangerous
thing to treat the Father's words lightly.

High-contriving Son of Themis of Straight Counsel:
this is not of your will nor of mine; yet I shall nail
you in bonds of indissoluble bronze on this crag far
from men. Here you shall hear no voice of mortal;   20
here you shall see no form of mortal. You shall be
grilled by the sun's bright fire and change the fair

bloom of your skin. You shall be glad when Night comes with her mantle of stars and hides the sun's light; but the sun shall scatter the hoarfrost again at dawn. Always the grievous burden of your torture will be there to wear you down; for he that shall cause it to cease has yet to be born.

Such is the reward you reap of your man-loving disposition. For you, a God, feared not the anger of the gods, but gave honor to mortals beyond what was just. Wherefore you shall mount guard on this unlovely rock, upright, sleepless, not bending the knee. Many a groan and many a lamentation you shall utter, but they shall not serve you. For the mind of Zeus is hard to soften with prayer, and every ruler is harsh whose rule is new. 30

Might
Come, why are you holding back? Why are you pitying in vain? Why is it that you do not hate a God whom the gods hate most of all? Why do you not hate him, since it was your honor that he betrayed to men?

Hephaestus
Our kinship has strange power; that, and our life together.

Might
Yes. But to turn a deaf ear to the Father's words— how can that be? Do you not fear that more? 40

Hephaestus
You are always pitiless, always full of ruthlessness.

Might
There is no good singing dirges over him. Do not labor uselessly at what helps not at all.

Hephaestus
O handicraft of mine—that I deeply hate!

Might
Why do you hate it? To speak simply, your craft is in no way the author of his present troubles.

Hephaestus
Yet would another had had this craft allotted to him.

Might
There is nothing without discomfort except the over-lordship of the gods. For only Zeus is free. 50

Hephaestus
I know. I have no answer to this.

Might
Hurry now. Throw the chain around him that the Father may not look upon your tarrying.

Hephaestus
There are the fetters, there: you can see them.

Might
Put them on his hands: strong, now with the hammer: strike. Nail him to the rock.

Hephaestus
It is being done now. I am not idling at my work.

Might
Hammer it more; put in the wedge; leave it loose nowhere. He's a cunning fellow at finding a way even out of hopeless difficulties.

Hephaestus
Look now, his arm is fixed immovably! 60

Might
Nail the other safe, that he may learn, for all his cleverness, that he is duller witted than Zeus.

Hephaestus
No one, save Prometheus, can justly blame me.

Might
Drive the obstinate jaw of the adamantine wedge
right through his breast: drive it hard.

Hephaestus
Alas, Prometheus, I groan for your sufferings.

Might
Are you pitying again? Are you groaning for the
enemies of Zeus? Have a care, lest some day you
may be pitying yourself.

Hephaestus
You see a sight that hurts the eye.

Might
I see this rascal getting his deserts. Throw the girth   70
around his sides.

Hephaestus
I am forced to do this; do not keep urging me.

Might
Yes, I will urge you, and hound you on as well. Get
below now, and hoop his legs in strongly.

Hephaestus
There now, the task is done. It has not taken long.

Might
Hammer the piercing fetters with all your power, for
the Overseer of our work is severe.

Hephaestus
Your looks and the refrain of your tongue are alike.

Might
You can be softhearted. But do not blame my stubbornness and harshness of temper.   80

Hephaestus
Let us go. He has the harness on his limbs.

Might (to Prometheus)
Now, play the insolent; now, plunder the gods' privileges and give them to creatures of a day. What drop
of your sufferings can mortals spare you? The gods
named you wrongly when they called you Forethought; you yourself *need* Forethought to extricate
yourself from this contrivance.

(*Prometheus is left alone on the rock.*)

Prometheus
Bright light, swift-winged winds, springs of the rivers,
   numberless
laughter of the sea's waves, earth, mother of all, and
   the all-seeing   90
circle of the sun: I call upon you to see what I, a
   God, suffer
at the hands of gods—
see with what kind of torture
worn down I shall wrestle ten thousand
years of time—
such is the despiteful bond that the Prince
has devised against me, the new Prince
of the Blessed Ones. Oh woe is me!
I groan for the present sorrow,
I groan for the sorrow to come, I groan
questioning when there shall come a time
when He shall ordain a limit to my sufferings.
What am I saying? I have known all before,   100
all that shall be, and clearly known; to me,
nothing that hurts shall come with a new face.
So must I bear, as lightly as I can,
the destiny that fate has given me;
for I know well against necessity,
against its strength, no one can fight and win.

I cannot speak about my fortune, cannot
hold my tongue either. It was mortal man
to whom I gave great privileges and

for that was yoked in this unyielding harness.
I hunted out the secret spring of fire,
that filled the narthex stem, which when revealed   110
became the teacher of each craft to men,
a great resource. This is the sin committed
for which I stand accountant, and I pay
nailed in my chains under the open sky.

Ah! Ah!
What sound, what sightless smell approaches me,
God sent, or mortal, or mingled?
Has it come to earth's end
to look on my sufferings,
or what does it wish?
You see me a wretched God in chains,   120
the enemy of Zeus, hated of all
the gods that enter Zeus's palace hall,
because of my excessive love for Man.
What is that? The rustle
of birds' wings near? The air whispers
with the gentle strokes of wings.
Everything that comes toward me is occasion for
     fear.

(*The Chorus, composed of the daughters of Oceanos,
     enters, the members wearing some formalized
          representation of wings, so that their
               general appearance is birdlike.*)

Chorus
Fear not: this is a company of friends
that comes to your mountain with swift
rivalry of wings.   130
Hardly had we persuaded our Father's
mind, and the quick-bearing winds
speeded us hither. The sound
of stroke of bronze rang through our cavern
in its depths and it shook from us

shamefaced modesty; unsandaled
we have hastened on our chariot of wings.

Prometheus
Alas, children of teeming Tethys and of him
who encircles all the world with stream unsleeping,
Father Ocean, 140
look, see with what chains
I am nailed on the craggy heights
of this gully to keep a watch
that none would envy me.

Chorus
I see, Prometheus: and a mist of fear and tears
besets my eyes as I see your form
wasting away on these cliffs
in adamantine bonds of bitter shame.
For new are the steersmen that rule Olympus:
and new are the customs by which Zeus rules,
customs that have no law to them, 150
but what was great before he brings to nothingness.

Prometheus
Would that he had hurled me
underneath the earth and underneath
the House of Hades, host to the dead—
yes, down to limitless Tartarus,
yes, though he bound me cruelly
in chains unbreakable,
so neither God nor any other being
might have found joy in gloating over me.
Now as I hang, the plaything of the winds,
my enemies can laugh at what I suffer.

Chorus
Who of the gods is so hard of heart 160
that he finds joy in this?
Who is that that does not feel
sorrow answering your pain—
save only Zeus? For he malignantly,

145

always cherishing a mind
that bends not, has subdued the breed
of Uranos, nor shall he cease
until he satisfies his heart,
or someone take the rule from him—that hard-to-
   capture rule—
by some device of subtlety.

Prometheus
Yes, there shall come a day for me
when he shall need me, me that now am tortured
in bonds and fetters—he shall need me then,
this president of the Blessed—   170
to show the new plot whereby he may be spoiled
of his throne and his power,
Then not with honeyed tongues
of persuasion shall he enchant me;
he shall not cow me with his threats
to tell him what I know,
until he free me from my cruel chains
and pay me recompense for what I suffer.

Chorus
You are stout of heart, unyielding   180
to the bitterness of pain.
You are free of tongue, too free.
It is my mind that piercing fear has fluttered;
your misfortunes frighten me.
Where and when is it fated
to see you reach the term, to see you reach
the harbor free of trouble at the last?
A disposition none can win, a heart
that no persuasions soften—these are his,
the Son of Kronos.

Prometheus
I know that he is savage: and his justice
a thing he keeps by his own standard: still
that will of his shall melt to softness yet   190

146

when he is broken in the way I know,
and though his temper now is oaken hard
it shall be softened: hastily he'll come
to meet my haste, to join in amity
and union with me—one day he shall come.

Chorus
Reveal it all to us: tell us the story of what the
charge was on which Zeus caught you and punished
you so cruelly with such dishonor. Tell us, if the
telling will not injure you in any way.

Prometheus
To speak of this is bitterness. To keep silent
bitter no less; and every way is misery.   200

When first the gods began their angry quarrel,
and God matched God in rising faction, some
eager to drive old Kronos from his throne
that Zeus might rule—the fools!—others again
earnest that Zeus might never be their king—
I then with the best counsel tried to win
the Titans, sons of Uranos and Earth,
but failed. They would have none of crafty schemes
and in their savage arrogance of spirit
thought they would lord it easily by force.   210
But she that was my mother, Themis, Earth—
she is but one although her names are many—
had prophesied to me how it should be,
even how the fates decreed it: and she said
that "not by strength nor overmastering force
the fates allowed the conquerors to conquer
but by guile only": This is what I told them,
but they would not vouchsafe a glance at me.
Then with those things before me it seemed best
to take my mother and join Zeus's side: 220
he was as willing as we were:
thanks to my plans the dark receptacle
of Tartarus conceals the ancient Kronos,

him and his allies. These were the services
I rendered to this tyrant and these pains
the payment he has given me in requital.
This is a sickness rooted and inherent
in the nature of a tyranny:
that he that holds it does not trust his friends.

But you have asked on what particular
charge he now tortures me: this I will tell you.
As soon as he ascended to the throne   230
that was his father's, straightway he assigned
to the several gods their several privileges
and portioned out the power, but to the unhappy
breed of mankind he gave no heed, intending
to blot the race out and create a new.
Against these plans none stood save I: I dared.
I rescued men from shattering destruction
that would have carried them to Hades' house;
and therefore I am tortured on this rock,
a bitterness to suffer, and a pain
to pitiful eyes. I gave to mortal man   240
a precedence over myself in pity: I
can win no pity: pitiless is he
that thus chastises me, a spectacle
bringing dishonor on the name of Zeus.

Chorus
He would be iron-minded and made of stone, indeed,
Prometheus, who did not sympathize with your sufferings. I would not have chosen to see them, and
now that I see, my heart is pained.

Prometheus
Yes, to my friends I am pitiable to see.

Chorus
Did you perhaps go further than you have told us?

Prometheus
I caused mortals to cease foreseeing doom.   250

Chorus
What cure did you provide them with against that sickness?

Prometheus
I placed in them blind hopes.

Chorus
That was a great gift you gave to men.

Prometheus
Besides this, I gave them fire.

Chorus
And do creatures of a day now possess bright-faced fire?

Prometheus
Yes, and from it they shall learn many crafts.

Chorus
Then these are the charges on which—

Prometheus
Zeus tortures me and gives me no respite.

Chorus
Is there no limit set for your pain?

Prometheus
None save when it shall seem good to Zeus.   260

Chorus
How will it ever seem good to him? What hope is there? Do you not see how you have erred? It is not pleasure for me to say that you have erred, and for you it is a pain to hear. But let us speak no more of all this and do you seek some means of deliverance from your trials.

Prometheus
It is an easy thing for one whose foot

is on the outside of calamity
to give advice and to rebuke the sufferer.
I have known all that you have said: I knew,
I knew when I transgressed nor will deny it.
In helping man I brought my troubles on me;
but yet I did not think that with such tortures 270
I should be wasted on these airy cliffs,
this lonely mountain top, with no one near.
But do not sorrow for my present suffering;
alight on earth and hear what is to come
that you may know the whole complete: I beg you
alight and join your sorrow with mine: misfortune
wandering the same track lights now upon one
and now upon another.

Chorus
                    Willing our ears,
that hear you cry to them, Prometheus, 280
now with light foot I leave the rushing car
and sky, the holy path of birds, and light
upon this jutting rock: I long
to hear your story to the end.

(*Enter Oceanos, riding on a hippocamp, or sea-
                                        monster.*)

Oceanos
                    I come
on a long journey, speeding past the boundaries,
to visit you, Prometheus: with the mind
alone, no bridle needed, I direct
my swift-winged bird; my heart is sore
for your misfortunes; you know that. I think 290
that it is kinship makes me feel them so.
Besides, apart from kinship, there is no one
I hold in higher estimation: that
you soon shall know and know beside that in me
there is no mere word-kindness: tell me
how I can help you, and you will never say

that you have any friend more loyal to you
than Oceanos.

Prometheus
What do I see? Have you, too, come to gape   300
in wonder at this great display, my torture?
How did you have the courage to come here
to this land, Iron-Mother, leaving the stream
called after you and the rock-roofed, self-established
caverns? Was it to feast your eyes upon
the spectacle of my suffering and join
in pity for my pain? Now look and see
the sight, this friend of Zeus, that helped set up
his tyranny and see what agonies
twist me, by his instructions!

Oceanos
                    Yes, I see,
Prometheus, and I want, indeed I do,
to advise you for the best, for all your cleverness.   310
Know yourself and reform your ways to new ways,
for new is he that rules among the Gods.
But if you throw about such angry words,
words that are whetted swords, soon Zeus will hear
    you,
even though his seat in glory is far removed,
and then your present multitude of pains
will seem like child's play. My poor friend, give up
this angry mood of yours and look for means
of getting yourself free of trouble. Maybe
what I say seems to you both old and commonplace;
but this is what you pay, Prometheus, for   320
that tongue of yours which talked so high and
    haughty:
you are not yet humble, still you do not yield
to your misfortunes, and you wish, indeed,
to add some more to them; now, if you follow
me as a schoolmaster you will not kick
against the pricks, seeing that he, the King,

that rules alone, is harsh and sends accounts
to no one's audit for the deeds he does.
Now I will go and try if I can free you:
do you be quiet, do not talk so much.
Since your mind is so subtle, don't you know   330
that a vain tongue is subject to correction?

Prometheus
I envy you, that you stand clear of blame,
yet shared and dared in everything with me!
Now let me be, and have no care for me.
Do what you will, Him you will not persuade;
He is not easily won over: look,
take care lest coming here to me should hurt you.

Oceanos
You are by nature better at advising
others than yourself. I take my cue
from deeds, not words. Do not withhold me now
when I am eager to go to Zeus. I'm sure,
I'm sure that he will grant this favor to me,   340
to free you from your chains.

Prometheus
I thank you and will never cease; for loyalty
is not what you are wanting in. Don't trouble,
for you will trouble to no purpose, and no help
to me—if it so be you want to trouble.
No, rest yourself, keep away from this thing;
because I am unlucky I would not,
for that, have everyone unlucky too.
No, for my heart is sore already when
I think about my brothers' fortunes—Atlas,   350
who stands to westward of the world, supporting
the pillar of earth and heaven on his shoulders,
a load that suits no shoulders; and the earthborn
dweller in caves Cilician, whom I saw
and pitied, hundred-headed, dreadful monster,

fierce Typho, conquered and brought low by force.
Once against all the gods he stood, opposing,
hissing out terror from his grim jaws; his eyes
flashed gorgon glaring lightning as he thought
to sack the sovereign tyranny of Zeus;
but upon him came the unsleeping bolt
of Zeus, the lightning-breathing flame, down rushing,　　360
which cast him from his high aspiring boast.
Struck to the heart, his strength was blasted dead
and burnt to ashes; now a sprawling mass
useless he lies, hard by the narrow seaway
pressed down beneath the roots of Aetna: high
above him on the mountain peak the smith
Hephaestus works at the anvil. Yet one day
there shall burst out rivers of fire, devouring
with savage jaws the fertile, level plains　　370
of Sicily of the fair fruits; such boiling wrath
with weapons of fire-breathing surf, a fiery
unapproachable torrent, shall Typho vomit,
though Zeus's lightning left him but a cinder.
But all of this you know: you do not need me
to be your schoolmaster: reassure yourself
as you know how: this cup I shall drain myself
till the high mind of Zeus shall cease from anger.

Oceanos
Do you not know, Prometheus, that words are healers
of the sick temper?　　380

Prometheus
Yes, if in season due one soothes the heart with
them, not tries violently to reduce the swelling anger.

Oceanos
Tell me, what danger do you see for me in loyalty to
you, and courage therein?

Prometheus
I see only useless effort and a silly good nature.

Oceanos
Suffer me then to be sick of this sickness, for it is a
profitable thing, if one is wise, to seem foolish.

Prometheus
This shall seem to be my fault.

Oceanos
Clearly your words send me home again.

Prometheus
Yes, lest your doings for me bring you enmity.   390

Oceanos
His enmity, who newly sits on the all-powerful
throne?

Prometheus
His is a heart you should beware of vexing.

Oceanos
Your own misfortune will be my teacher, Prometheus.

Prometheus
Off with you, then! Begone! Keep your present mind.

Oceanos
These words fall on very responsive ears. Already my
four-legged bird is pawing the level track of Heaven
with his wings, and he will be glad to bend the knee
in his own stable.

Chorus
STROPHE
I cry aloud, Prometheus, and lament your bitter fate,
my tender eyes are trickling tears: 400
their fountains wet my cheek.
This is a tyrant's deed; this is unlovely,
a thing done by a tyrant's private laws,
and with this thing Zeus shows his haughtiness
of temper toward the gods that were of old.

ANTISTROPHE

Now all the earth has cried aloud, lamenting:
now all that was magnificent of old
laments your fall, laments your brethren's fall   410
as many as in holy Asia hold
their stablished habitation, all lament
in sympathy for your most grievous woes.

STROPHE

Dwellers in the land of Colchis,
maidens, fearless in the fight,
and the host of Scythia, living
round the lake Maeotis, living
on the edges of the world.

ANTISTROPHE

And Arabia's flower of warriors   420
and the craggy fortress keepers
near Caucasian mountains, fighters
terrible, crying for battle,
brandishing sharp pointed spears.

STROPHE

One God and one God only I have seen
before this day, in torture and in bonds
unbreakable: he was a Titan,
Alas, whose strength and might
ever exceeded; now he bends his back
and groans beneath the load of earth and heaven.   430

— ANTISTROPHE

The wave cries out as it breaks into surf;
the depth cries out, lamenting you; the dark
Hades, the hollow underneath the world,
sullenly groans below; the springs
of sacred flowing rivers all lament
the pain and pity of your suffering.

Prometheus
Do not think that out of pride or stubbornness I hold

my peace; my heart is eaten away when I am aware
of myself, when I see myself insulted as I am. Who
was it but I who in truth dispensed their honors to
these new gods? I will say nothing of this; you know   440
it all; but hear what troubles there were among men,
how I found them witless and gave them the use of
their wits and made them masters of their minds. I
will tell you this, not because I would blame men, but
to explain the goodwill of my gift. For men at first
had eyes but saw to no purpose; they had ears but
did not hear. Like the shapes of dreams they dragged
through their long lives and handled all things in
bewilderment and confusion. They did not know of
building houses with bricks to face the sun; they did
not know how to work in wood. They lived like
swarming ants in holes in the ground, in the sunless
caves of the earth. For them there was no secure   450
token by which to tell winter nor the flowering spring
nor the summer with its crops; all their doings were
indeed without intelligent calculation until I showed
them the rising of the stars, and the settings, hard to
observe. And further I discovered to them numbering,
pre-eminent among subtle devices, and the combining   460
of letters as a means of remembering all things, the
Muses' mother, skilled in craft. It was I who first
yoked beasts for them in the yokes and made of those
beasts the slaves of trace chain and pack saddle that
they might be man's substitute in the hardest tasks;
and I harnessed to the carriage, so that they loved the
rein, horses, the crowning pride of the rich man's
luxury. It was I and none other who discovered ships,
the sail-driven wagons that the sea buffets. Such were
the contrivances that I discovered for men—alas for
me! For I myself am without contrivance to rid myself   470
of my present affliction.

Chorus
What you have suffered is indeed terrible. You are all

astray and bewildered in your mind, and like a bad
doctor that has fallen sick himself, you are cast down
and cannot find what sort of drugs would cure your
ailment.

Prometheus

Hear the rest, and you will marvel even more at the
crafts and resources I contrived. Greatest was this: in
the former times if a man fell sick he had no defense
against the sickness, neither healing food nor drink,
nor unguent; but through the lack of drugs men   480
wasted away, until I showed them the blending of
mild simples wherewith they drive out all manner of
diseases. It was I who arranged all the ways of seer-
craft, and I first adjudged what things come verily
true from dreams; and to men I gave meaning to the
ominous cries, hard to interpret. It was I who set in
order the omens of the highway and the flight of
crooked-taloned birds, which of them were propitious   490
or lucky by nature, and what manner of life each led,
and what were their mutual hates, loves, and com-
panionships; also I taught of the smoothness of the
vitals and what color they should have to pleasure
the gods and the dappled beauty of the gall and the
lobe. It was I who burned thighs wrapped in fat and
the long shank bone and set mortals on the road to
this murky craft. It was I who made visible to men's
eyes the flaming signs of the sky that were before
dim. So much for these. Beneath the earth, man's   500
hidden blessing, copper, iron, silver, and gold—will
anyone claim to have discovered these before I did?
No one, I am very sure, who wants to speak truly and
to the purpose. One brief word will tell the whole
story: all arts that mortals have come from Prometheus.

Chorus

Therefore do not help mortals beyond all expediency
while neglecting yourself in your troubles. For I am

of good hope that once freed of these bonds you will
be no less in power than Zeus.   510

Prometheus
Not yet has fate that brings to fulfilment determined
these things to be thus. I must be twisted by ten
thousand pangs and agonies, as I now am, to escape
my chains at last. Craft is far weaker than necessity.

Chorus
Who then is the steersman of necessity?

Prometheus
The triple-formed Fates and the remembering Furies.

Chorus
Is Zeus weaker than these?

Prometheus
Yes, for he, too, cannot escape what is fated.

Chorus
What is fated for Zeus besides eternal sovereignty?

Prometheus
Inquire of this no further, do not entreat me.   520

Chorus
This is some solemn secret, I suppose, that you are
hiding.

Prometheus
Think of some other story: this one it is not yet the
season to give tongue to, but it must be hidden with
all care; for it is only by keeping it that I will escape
my despiteful bondage and my agony.

Chorus
STROPHE
May Zeus never, Zeus that all
the universe controls, oppose
his power against my mind:

158

may I never dallying
be slow to give my worship at   530
the sacrificial feasts
when the bulls are killed beside
quenchless Father Ocean:
may I never sin in word:
may these precepts still abide
in my mind nor melt away.

ANTISTROPHE

It is a sweet thing to draw out
a long, long life in cheerful hopes,
and feed the spirit in the bright
benignity of happiness:
but I shiver when I see you   540
wasted with ten thousand pains,
all because you did not tremble
at the name of Zeus: your mind
was yours, not his, and at its bidding
you regarded mortal men
too high, Prometheus.

STROPHE

Kindness that cannot be requited, tell me,
where is the help in that, my friend? What succor
in creatures of a day? You did not see
the feebleness that draws its breath in gasps,
a dreamlike feebleness by which the race   550
of man is held in bondage, a blind prisoner.
So the plans of men shall never
pass the ordered law of Zeus.

ANTISTROPHE

This I have learned while I looked on your pains,
deadly pains, Prometheus.
A dirge for you came to my lips, so different
from the other song I sang to crown your marriage
in honor of your couching and your bath,

upon the day you won her with your gifts
to share your bed—of your own race she was,
Hesione—and so you brought her home.   560

(*Enter Io, a girl wearing horns like an ox.*)

Io
What land is this? what race of men? Who is it
I see here tortured in this rocky bondage?
What is the sin he's paying for? Oh tell me
to what part of the world my wanderings have
    brought me.
O, O, O,
there it is again, there again—it stings me,
the gadfly, the ghost of earth-born Argos:
keep it away, keep it away, earth!
I'm frightened when I see the shape of Argos,
Argos the herdsman with ten thousand eyes.   570
He stalks me with his crafty eyes: he died,
but the earth didn't hide him; still he comes
even from the depths of the Underworld to hunt me:
he drives me starving by the sands of the sea.

The reed-woven pipe drones on in a hum
and drones and drones its sleep-giving strain:
O, O, O,
Where are you bringing me, my far-wandering wan-
    derings?
Son of Kronos, what fault, what fault
did you find in me that you should yoke me
to a harness of misery like this,
that you should torture me so to madness   580
driven in fear of the gadfly?
Burn me with fire: hide me in earth: cast me away
to monsters of the deep for food: but do not
grudge me the granting of this prayer, King.
Enough have my much wandering wanderings
exercised me: I cannot find

a way to escape my troubles.
Do you hear the voice of the cow-horned maid?

Prometheus

Surely I hear the voice, the voice of the maiden,
gadfly-haunted, the daughter of Inachus? She set   590
Zeus's heart on fire with love and now she is violently
exercised running on courses overlong, driven by
Hera's hate.

Io

How is it you speak my father's name?
Tell me, who are you? Who are you? Oh
who are you that so exactly accosts me by name?
You have spoken of the disease that the gods have
    sent to me
which wastes me away, pricking with goads,
so that I am moving always
tortured and hungry, wild bounding,
quick sped I come,   600
a victim of jealous plots.
Some have been wretched
before me, but who of these
suffered as I do?
But declare to me clearly
what I have still to suffer: what would avail
against my sickness, what drug would cure it:
Tell me, if you know:
tell me, declare it to the unlucky, wandering maid.

Prometheus

I shall tell you clearly all that you would know,
weaving you no riddles, but in plain words, as it is
just to open the lips to friends. You see before you   610
him that gave fire to men, even Prometheus.

Io

O spirit that has appeared as a common blessing to
all men, unhappy Prometheus, why are you being
punished?

Prometheus
I have just this moment ceased from the lamentable
tale of my sorrows.

Io
Will you then grant me this favor?

Prometheus
Say what you are asking for: I will tell you all.

Io
Tell who it was that nailed you to the cliff.

Prometheus
The plan was the plan of Zeus, and the hand the
hand of Hephaestus.

Io
And what was the offense of which this is the
punishment?   620

Prometheus
It is enough that I have told you a clear story so far.

Io
In addition, then, indicate to me what date shall be
the limit of my wanderings.

Prometheus
Better for you not to know this than know it.

Io
I beg you, do not hide from me what I must endure.

Prometheus
It is not that I grudge you this favor.

Io
Why then delay to tell me all?

Prometheus
It is no grudging, but I hesitate to break your spirit.

Io

Do not have more thought for me than pleases me
myself.

Prometheus

Since you are so eager, I must speak; and do you
give ear.   630

Chorus

Not yet: give me, too, a share of pleasure. First let us
question her concerning her sickness, and let her tell
us of her desperate fortunes. And then let you be our
informant for the sorrows that still await her.

Prometheus

It is your task, Io, to gratify these spirits, for besides
other considerations they are your father's sisters. To
make wail and lament for one's ill fortune, when one
will win a tear from the audience, is well worthwhile.

Io

I know not how I should distrust you: clearly   640
you shall hear all you want to know from me.
Yet even as I speak I groan in bitterness
for that storm sent by God on me, that ruin
of my beauty; I must sorrow when I think
who sent all this upon me. There were always
night visions that kept haunting me and coming
into my maiden chamber and exhorting
with winning words, "O maiden greatly blessed,
why are you still a maiden, you who might
make marriage with the greatest? Zeus is stricken
with lust for you; he is afire to try   650
the bed of love with you: do not disdain him.
Go, child, to Lerna's meadow, deep in grass,
to where your father's flocks and cattle stand
that Zeus's eye may cease from longing for you."
With such dreams I was cruelly beset
night after night until I took the courage
to tell my father of my nightly terror.

He sent to Pytho many an embassy
and to Dodona seeking to discover
what deed or word of his might please the God,   660
but those he sent came back with riddling oracles
dark and beyond the power of understanding.
At last the word came clear to Inachus
charging him plainly that he cast me out
of home and country, drive me out footloose
to wander to the limits of the world;
if he should not obey, the oracle said,
the fire-faced thunderbolt would come from Zeus
and blot out his whole race. These were the oracles
of Loxias, and Inachus obeyed them.   670
He drove me out and shut his doors against me
with tears on both our parts, but Zeus's bit
compelled him to do this against his will.
Immediately my form and mind were changed
and all distorted; horned, as you see,
pricked on by the sharp biting gadfly, leaping
in frenzied jumps I ran beside the river
Kerchneia, good to drink, and Lerna's spring.
The earth-born herdsman Argos followed me
whose anger knew no limits, and he spied   680
after my tracks with all his hundred eyes.
Then an unlooked-for doom, descending suddenly,
took him from life: I, driven by the gadfly,
that god-sent scourge, was driven always onward
from one land to another: that is my story.
If you can tell me what remains for me,
tell me, and do not out of pity cozen
with kindly lies: there is no sickness worse
for me than words that to be kind must lie.

Chorus
Hold! Keep away! Alas!
never did I think that such strange
words would come to my ears:
never did I think such intolerable   690

164

sufferings, an offense to the eye,
shameful and frightening, so
would chill my soul with a double-edged point.
Alas, Alas, for your fate!
I shudder when I look on Io's fortune.

Prometheus
You groan too soon: you are full of fear too soon:
wait till you hear besides what is to be.

Chorus
Speak, tell us to the end. For sufferers it is sweet to
know beforehand clearly the pain that still remains
for them.

Prometheus
The first request you made of me you gained   700
lightly: from her you wished to hear the story
of what she suffered. Now hear what remains,
what sufferings this maid must yet endure
from Hera. Do you listen, child of Inachus,
hear and lay up my words within your heart
that you may know the limits of your journey.
First turn to the sun's rising and walk on
over the fields no plough has broken: then
you will come to the wandering Scythians
who live in wicker houses built above
their well-wheeled wagons; they are an armed people,   710
armed with the bow that strikes from far away:
do not draw near them; rather let your feet
touch the surf line of the sea where the waves moan,
and cross their country: on your left there live
the Chalybes who work with iron: these
you must beware of; for they are not gentle,
nor people whom a stranger dare approach.
Then you will come to Insolence, a river
that well deserves its name: but cross it not—
it is no stream that you can easily ford—

until you come to Caucasus itself,
the highest mountains, where the river's strength   720
gushes from its very temples. Cross these peaks,
the neighbors of the stars, and take the road
southward until you reach the Amazons,
the race of women who hate men, who one day
shall live around Thermodon in Themiscyra
where Salmydessos, rocky jaw of the sea,
stands sailor-hating, stepmother of ships.
The Amazons will set you on your way
and gladly: you will reach Cimmeria,
the isthmus, at the narrow gates of the lake.   730
Leave this with a good heart and cross the channel,
the channel of Maeotis: and hereafter
for all time men shall talk about your crossing,
and they shall call the place for you Cow's-ford.*
Leave Europe's mainland then, and go to Asia.

(To the Chorus)
Do you now think this tyrant of the gods
is hard in all things without difference?
He was a God and sought to lie in love
with this girl who was mortal, and on her
he brought this curse of wandering: bitter indeed
you found your marriage with this suitor, maid.
Yet you must think of all that I have told you
as still only in prelude.   740

Io
O, O

Prometheus
Again, you are crying and lamenting: what will you
do when you hear of the evils to come?

Chorus
Is there still something else to her sufferings of which
you will speak?

-----

ford: Bosporus.

Prometheus
A wintry sea of agony and ruin.

Io
What good is life to me then? Why do I not throw myself at once from some rough crag, to strike the ground and win a quittance of all my troubles? It 750
would be better to die once for all than suffer all one's days.

Prometheus
You would ill bear my trials, then, for whom Fate reserves no death. Death would be a quittance of trouble: but for me there is no limit of suffering set till Zeus fall from power.

Io
Can Zeus ever fall from power?

Prometheus
You would be glad to see that catastrophe, I think.

Io
Surely, since Zeus is my persecutor.

Prometheus
Then know that this shall be. 760

Io
Who will despoil him of his sovereign scepter?

Prometheus
His own witless plans.

Io
How? Tell me, if there is no harm to telling.

Prometheus
He shall make a marriage that shall hurt him.

Io
With god or mortal? Tell me, if you may say it.

Prometheus
Why ask what marriage? That is not to be spoken.

Io
Is it his wife shall cast him from his throne?

Prometheus
She shall bear him a son mightier than his father.

Io
Has he no possibility of escaping this downfall?

Prometheus
None, save through my release from these chains.   770

Io
But who will free you, against Zeus's will?

Prometheus
Fate has determined that it be one of your descendants.

Io
What, shall a child of mine bring you free?

Prometheus
Yes, in the thirteenth generation.

Io
Your prophecy has now passed the limits of understanding.

Prometheus
Then also do not seek to learn your trials.

Io
Do not offer me a boon and then withhold it.

Prometheus
I offer you then one of two stories.

Io
Which? Tell me and give me the choice.

Prometheus

I will: choose that I tell you clearly either what   780
remains for you or the one that shall deliver me.

Chorus

Grant her one and grant me the other and do not
deny us the tale. Tell her what remains of her
wanderings: tell us of the one that shall deliver you.
That is what I desire.

Prometheus

Since you have so much eagerness, I will not
refuse to tell you all that you have asked me.
First to you, Io, I shall tell the tale
of your sad wanderings, rich in groans—inscribe
the story in the tablets of your mind.   790
When you shall cross the channel that divides
Europe from Asia, turn to the rising sun,
to the burnt plains, sun-scorched; cross by the edge
of the foaming sea till you come to Gorgona
to the flat stretches of Kisthene's country.
There live the ancient maids, children of Phorcys:
these swan-formed hags, with but one common eye,
single-toothed monsters, such as nowhere else
the sun's rays look on nor the moon by night.
Near are their winged sisters, the three Gorgons,
with snakes to bind their hair up, mortal-hating: 800
nor mortal that but looks on them shall live:
these are the sentry guards I tell you of.
Hear, too, of yet another gruesome sight,
the sharp-toothed hounds of Zeus, that have no bark,
the vultures—them take heed of—and the host
of one-eyed Arimaspians, horse-riding,
that live around the spring which flows with gold,
the spring of Pluto's river: go not near them.
A land far off, a nation of black men,
these you shall come to, men who live hard by
the fountain of the sun where is the river
Aethiops—travel by his banks along   810

to a waterfall where from the Bibline hills
Nile pours his holy waters, pure to drink.
This river shall be your guide to the triangular
land of the Nile and there, by Fate's decree,
there, Io, you shall find your distant home,
a colony for you and your descendants.
If anything of this is still obscure
or difficult ask me again and learn
clearly: I have more leisure than I wish.

Chorus
If there is still something left for you to tell her of
her ruinous wanderings, tell it; but if you have said   820
everything, grant us the favor we asked and tell us
the story too.

Prometheus
The limit of her wanderings complete
she now has heard: but so that she may know
that she has not been listening to no purpose
I shall recount what she endured before
she came to us here: this I give as pledge,
a witness to the good faith of my words.
The great part of the story I omit
and come to the very boundary of your travels.
When you had come to the Molossian plains
around the sheer back of Dodona where   830
is the oracular seat of Zeus Thesprotian,
the talking oaks, a wonder past belief,
by them full clearly, in no riddling terms,
you were hailed glorious wife of Zeus that shall be:
does anything of this wake pleasant memories?
Then, goaded by the gadfly, on you hastened
to the great gulf of Rhea by the track
at the side of the sea: but in returning course
you were storm-driven back: in time to come
that inlet of the sea shall bear your name
and shall be called Ionian, a memorial   840
to all men of your journeying: these are proofs

for you, of how far my mind sees something farther
than what is visible: for what is left,
to you and you this I shall say in common,
taking up again the track of my old tale.
There is a city, furthest in the world,
Canobos, near the mouth and issuing point
of the Nile: there Zeus shall make you sound of mind
touching you with a hand that brings no fear,
and through that touch alone shall come your healing.   850
You shall bear Epaphos, dark of skin, his name
recalling Zeus's touch and his begetting.
This Epaphos shall reap the fruit of all
the land that is watered by the broad flowing Nile.
From him five generations, and again
to Argos they shall come, against their will,
in number fifty, women, flying from
a marriage with their kinsfolk: but these kinsfolk
their hearts with lust aflutter like the hawks
barely outdistanced by the doves will come
hunting a marriage that the law forbids:
the God shall grudge the men these women's bodies,
and the Pelasgian earth shall welcome them   860
in death: for death shall claim them in a fight
where women strike in the dark, a murderous vigil.
Each wife shall rob her husband of his life
dipping in blood her two-edged sword: even so
may Love come, too, upon my enemies.
But one among these girls shall love beguile
from killing her bedfellow, blunting her purpose:
and she shall make her choice—to bear the name
of coward and not murder: this girl,
she shall in Argos bear a race of kings.
To tell this clearly needs a longer story,   870
but from her seed shall spring a man renowned
for archery, and he shall set me free.
Such was the prophecy which ancient Themis
my Titan mother opened up to me;
but how and by what means it shall come true

would take too long to tell, and if you heard
the knowledge would not profit you.

Io
Eleleu, eleleu
It creeps on me again, the twitching spasm,
the mind-destroying madness, burning me up
and the gadfly's sting goads me on—
steel point by no fire tempered—   880
and my heart in its fear knocks on my breast.
There's a dazing whirl in my eyes as I run
out of my course by the madness driven,
the crazy frenzy; my tongue ungoverned
babbles, the words in a muddy flow strike
on the waves of the mischief I hate, strike wild
without aim or sense.

Chorus
STROPHE
A wise man indeed he was
that first in judgment weighed this word
and gave it tongue: the best by far
it is to marry in one's rank and station: 890
let no one working with her hands aspire
to marriage with those lifted high in pride
because of wealth, or of ancestral glory.

ANTISTROPHE
Never, never may you see me,
Fates majestic, drawing nigh
the bed of Zeus, to share it with the kings:
nor ever may I know a heavenly wooer:
I dread such things beholding
Io's sad virginity
ravaged, ruined; bitter wandering
hers because of Hera's wrath.   900

EPODE
When a match has equal partners
then I fear not: may the eye

inescapable of the mighty
gods not look on me.
That is a fight that none can fight: a fruitful
source of fruitlessness: I would not
know what I could do: I cannot
see the hope when Zeus is angry
of escaping him.

Prometheus
Yet shall this Zeus, for all his pride of heart
be humble yet: such is the match he plans,
a marriage that shall drive him from his power
and from his throne, out of the sight of all.   910
So shall at last the final consummation
be brought about of Father Kronos' curse
which he, driven from his ancient throne, invoked
against the son deposing him: no one
of all the gods save I alone can tell
a way to escape this mischief: I alone
know it and how. So let him confidently
sit on his throne and trust his heavenly thunder
and brandish in his hand his fiery bolt.
Nothing shall all of this avail against   920
a fall intolerable, a dishonored end.
So strong a wrestler Zeus is now equipping
against himself, a monster hard to fight.
This enemy shall find a plan to best
the thunderbolt, a thunderclap to best
the thunderclap of Zeus: and he shall shiver
Poseidon's trident, curse of sea and land.
So, in his crashing fall shall Zeus discover
how different are rule and slavery.

Chorus
You voice your wishes for the God's destruction.

Prometheus
They are my wishes, yet shall come to pass.

Chorus
Must we expect someone to conquer Zeus?   930

Prometheus
Yes; he shall suffer worse than I do now.

Chorus
Have you no fear of uttering such words?

Prometheus
Why should I fear, since death is not my fate?

Chorus
But he might give you pain still worse than this.

Prometheus
Then let him do so; all this I expect.

Chorus
Wise are the worshipers of Adrasteia.

Prometheus
Worship him, pray; flatter whatever king
is king today; but I care less than nothing
for Zeus. Let him do what he likes,
let him be king for his short time: he shall not   940
be king for long.
                  Look, here is Zeus's footman,
this fetch-and-carry messenger of him,
the New King. Certainly he has come here
with news for us.

Hermes
                  You, subtle-spirit, you
bitterly overbitter, you that sinned
against the immortals, giving honor to
the creatures of a day, you thief of fire:
the Father has commanded you to say
what marriage of his is this you brag about
that shall drive him from power—and declare it   950
in clear terms and no riddles. You, Prometheus,
do not cause me a double journey; these

174

(Pointing to the chains.)

will prove to you that Zeus is not softhearted.

Prometheus
Your speech is pompous sounding, full of pride,
as fits the lackey of the gods. You are young
and young your rule and you think that the tower
in which you live is free from sorrow: from it
have I not seen two tyrants thrown? the third,
who now is king, I shall yet live to see him
fall, of all three most suddenly, most dishonored.
Do you think I will crouch before your gods,   960
—so new—and tremble? I am far from that.
Hasten away, back on the road you came.
You shall learn nothing that you ask of me.

Hermes
Just such the obstinacy that brought you here,
to this self-willed calamitous anchorage.

Prometheus
Be sure of this: when I set my misfortune
against your slavery, I would not change.

Hermes
It is better, I suppose, to be a slave
to this rock, than Zeus's trusted messenger.

Prometheus
Thus must the insolent show their insolence!   970

Hermes
I think you find your present lot too soft.

Prometheus
Too soft? I would my enemies had it then,
and you are one of those I count as such.

Hermes
Oh, you would blame me too for your calamity?

Prometheus
In a single word, I am the enemy
of all the gods that gave me ill for good.

Hermes
Your words declare you mad, and mad indeed.

Prometheus
Yes, if it's madness to detest my foes.

Hermes
No one could bear you in success.

Prometheus
                            Alas!

Hermes
Alas! *Zeus* does not know that word.   980

Prometheus
Time in its aging course teaches all things.

Hermes
But you have not yet learned a wise discretion.

Prometheus
True: or I would not speak so to a servant.

Hermes
It seems you will not grant the Father's wish.

Prometheus
I should be glad, indeed, to requite his kindness!

Hermes
You mock me like a child!

Prometheus
                 And are you not
a child, and sillier than a child, to think
that I should tell you anything? There is not
a torture or an engine wherewithal
Zeus can induce me to declare these things,   990
till he has loosed me from these cruel shackles.

So let him hurl his smoky lightning flame,
and throw in turmoil all things in the world
with white-winged snowflakes and deep bellowing
thunder beneath the earth: me he shall not
bend by all this to tell him who is fated
to drive him from his tyranny.

Hermes
Think, here and now, if this seems to your interest.

Prometheus
I have already thought—and laid my plans.

Hermes
Bring your proud heart to know a true discretion—
O foolish spirit—in the face of ruin.   1000

Prometheus
You vex me by these senseless adjurations,
senseless as if you were to advise the waves.
Let it not cross your mind that I will turn
womanish-minded from my fixed decision
or that I shall entreat the one I hate
so greatly, with a woman's upturned hands,
to loose me from my chains: I am far from that.

Hermes
I have said too much already—so I think—
and said it to no purpose: you are not softened:
your purpose is not dented by my prayers.
You are a colt new broken, with the bit   1010
clenched in its teeth, fighting against the reins,
and bolting. You are far too strong and confident
in your weak cleverness. For obstinacy
standing alone is the weakest of all things
in one whose mind is not possessed by wisdom.
Think what a storm, a triple wave of ruin
will rise against you, if you will not hear me,
and no escape for you. First this rough crag
with thunder and the lightning bolt the Father

shall cleave asunder, and shall hide your body
wrapped in a rocky clasp within its depth;
a tedious length of time you must fulfil   1020
before you see the light again, returning.
Then Zeus's winged hound, the eagle red,
shall tear great shreds of flesh from you, a feaster
coming unbidden, every day: your liver
bloodied to blackness will be his repast.
And of this pain do not expect an end
until some God shall show himself successor
to take your tortures for himself and willing
go down to lightless Hades and the shadows
of Tartarus' depths. Bear this in mind
and so determine. This is no feigned boast   1030
but spoken with too much truth. The mouth of Zeus
does not know how to lie, but every word
brings to fulfilment. Look, you, and reflect
and never think that obstinacy is better
than prudent counsel.

Chorus
                         Hermes seems to us
to speak not altogether out of season.
He bids you leave your obstinacy and seek
a wise good counsel. Hearken to him. Shame
it were for one so wise to fall in error.

Prometheus
Before he told it me I knew this message: 1040
but there is no disgrace in suffering
at an enemy's hand, when you hate mutually.
So let the curling tendril of the fire
from the lightning bolt be sent against me: let
the air be stirred with thunderclaps, the winds
in savage blasts convulsing all the world.
Let earth to her foundations shake, yes to her root,
before the quivering storm: let it confuse
the paths of heavenly stars and the sea's waves
in a wild surging torrent: this my body

let Him raise up on high and dash it down   1050
into black Tartarus with rigorous
compulsive eddies: death he cannot give me.

Hermes

These are a madman's words, a madman's plan:
is there a missing note in this mad harmony?
is there a slack chord in his madness? You,
you, who are so sympathetic with his troubles,
away with you from here, quickly away!   1060
lest you should find your wits stunned by the thunder
and its hard defending roar.

Chorus

                              Say something else
different from this: give me some other counsel
that I will listen to: this word of yours
for all its instancy is not for us.
How dare you bid us practice baseness? We
will bear along with him what we must bear.
I have learned to hate all traitors: there is no
disease I spit on more than treachery.   1070

Hermes

Remember then my warning before the act:
when you are trapped by ruin don't blame fortune.
Don't say that Zeus has brought you to calamity
that you could not foresee: do not do this:
but blame yourselves: now you know what you're
    doing:
and with this knowledge neither suddenly
nor secretly your own want of good sense
has tangled you in the net of ruin, past
all hope of rescue.

Prometheus

Now it is words no longer: now in very truth   1080
the earth is staggered: in its depths the thunder
bellows resoundingly, the fiery tendrils
of the lightning flash light up, and whirling clouds

carry the dust along: all the winds' blasts
dance in a fury one against the other
in violent confusion: earth and sea
are one, confused together: such is the storm
that comes against me manifestly from Zeus
to work its terrors. O Holy mother mine,   1090
O Sky that circling brings the light to all,
you see me, how I suffer, how unjustly.